Free Verse Editions

Edited by Jon Thompson

Free Verse Editions

Edited by Jon Thompson

2008

Quarry by Carolyn Guinzio
Between the Twilight and the Sky by Jennie Neighbors
The Prison Poems by Miguel Hernández,
      translated by Michael Smith
remanence by Boyer Rickel
What Stillness Illuminated by Yermiyahu Ahron Taub

2007

Child in the Road by Cindy Savett
Verge by Morgan Lucas Schuldt
The Flying House by Dawn-Michelle Baude

2006

Physis by Nicolas Pesque, translated by Cole Swensen
Puppet Wardrobe by Daniel Tiffany
These Beautiful Limits by Thomas Lisk
The Wash by Adam Clay

2005

A Map of Faring by Peter Riley
Signs Following by Ger Killeen
Winter Journey [Viaggio d'inverno] by Attilio Bertolucci,
      translated by Nicholas Benson

The Prison Poems

Miguel Hernández

Translated & Introduced

by

Michael Smith

Parlor Press
West Lafayette, Indiana
www.parlorpress.com

Parlor Press LLC, West Lafayette, Indiana 47906

Library of Congress Cataloging-in-Publication Data

Hernández, Miguel, 1910-1942
  [Cancionero y romancero de ausencias. English]
  The prison poems / Miguel Hernandez ; translated & introduced by Michael Smith.
      p. cm. -- (Free verse editions)
  Includes bibliographical references.
  ISBN 978-1-60235-090-8 (pbk. : alk. paper) -- ISBN 978-1-60235-091-5 (adobe ebook)
  1. Hernández, Miguel, 1910-1942--Translations into English. I. Smith, Michael, 1942 Sept. 1- II. Title.
  PQ6615.E57C2813 2008
  861'.62--dc22

                              2008048384

Printed in the United States of America
S A N: 2 5 4 - 8 8 7 9

Printed on acid-free paper.

Parlor Press, LLC is an independent publisher of scholarly and trade titles in print and multimedia formats. This book is available in paper and Adobe eBook formats from Parlor Press on the World Wide Web at http://www.parlorpress.com or through online and brick-and-mortar bookstores. For submission information or to find out about Parlor Press publications, write to Parlor Press, 816 Robinson St., West Lafayette, Indiana, 47906, or e-mail editor@ parlorpress.com.

Contents

Miguel Hernández:
A Poet of the People

Michael Smith

AN INTRODUCTION

The development of the poetry of Miguel Hernández, from its first book publication in *Perito en lunas* (*Skilled in Moons*, 1933) to his final poems collected in *Cancionero y romancero de ausencias* (*Song and Ballad Book of Absences*, 1938–1941), traces, in an extraordinary parallelism, the development of the man's sociopolitical concerns. In broad outline, that development is from a politically naive pastoralism, *Perito en lunas*, and love poetry, *El rayo que no cesa* (*Unceasing Lightning*), to an intensely political, even propagandist poetry, *Viento del pueblo* (*Wind of The People*), and then on to the final poems which ponder the meaning of the individual caught up in a huge and complex social and political upheaval (the Spanish Civil War). The poetic achievement of Hernández, it seems to me, lies in his winning through all the various purposes to which he devoted his poetic talent, and persisting to achieve the profound expression of an individualism that was tortured by the social and political concerns from which his humanity could not turn away.

———

Hernández's background is of considerable importance in understanding the development of his social concerns. He was born on October 30 in 1910 in the town of Orihuela in the province of Alicante. His father was a small-time goat-herd and dealer in goats and other livestock; a tough individual, he was strict and authoritarian. Hernández's mother was a quiet and affectionate woman who, as best she could, softened her husband's harsh domestic regime.

From childhood Hernández had to play his part in tending the goats in the fields and sierras of Orihuela. Thus early, direct and intimate contact with the world of nature, of animals and plants and weather, and their interactions, left an indelible impression on him. As he expressed this in his second book of poems, *El rayo que no cesa:*

> *Me llamo barro aunque Miguel me llame.*
> *Barro es mi profesión y mi destino:*
> *que mancha con su lengua cuanto lame.*

> [I am called clay though my name is Miguel.
> Clay is my profession and my destiny:
> it stains with its tongue whatever it licks.]

This identification of himself with the organic world of nature was to provide an emotional basis for his identification with the broad mass of humanity which lived, especially in the Spain of his time, so close to that world of nature. Hernández had an intimate relationship with the natural world and in his work he often celebrated what he saw as the majesty of nature and he passionately observed its countless mysteries. In one of his early poems 'Canto exaltado de amor a la naturaleza' ('Exalted Love Song to Nature') he refers to nature as *fontana de belleza* ('fountain of beauty'). Hernández had a deep and lasting connection with his native soil:

> *En mi tierra moriré*
> *entre la raíz y el grano*
> *que es tan mía por la mano*
> *como mía por el pie*

> [I shall die in my land
> among the root and the grain
> which is as much mine by its hand
> as it's mine by its foot.]

Spain in Hernández's time was predominantly a peasant society, with countless peasants living in a sort of feudal serfdom. The Irish poet, Patrick Kavanagh, has defined the 'peasant' as 'someone who lives below a certain threshold of consciousness'. Although Kavanagh unfortunately never went on to define what he understood as that level of consciousness, one can guess that what he meant was *individual* consciousness, that sense of being oneself, of being different and unique, the cherished concept of bourgeois life. Hernández, however, was able to identify with the Spanish peasant on a profoundly spiritual level:

> *Me vistió la pobreza,*
> *me lamió el cuerpo el río*
> *y del pie a la cabeza*
> *pasto fui del rocío.*

> [Poverty dressed me,
> the river lapped my body
> and from foot to head
> I was pasture of the dew.]

Hernández was not so much a political poet as a poet deeply concerned with social justice. He had an enlightened and active social conscience which led him very often to contemplate social problems, particularly those which affected Spain's rural labourers. He was a man of the people, always placing the needs of the poor and oppressed before the demands of any ambitious political organization or party. In his poetry he glorifies the worker and extols the virtues of honest, hard work:

> *Se tomará un descanso el hortelano*
> *y entenderá sus penas combatido*
> *por el salubre sol y el tiempo manso.*

> *Y otra vez, inclinando cuerpo y mano*
> *seguirá ante la tierra perseguido*
> *por la sombra del último descanso.*

> [The gardener will take his rest
> and he will understand his pains, beaten
> by the healthful sun and mild weather.

> And again, inclining his body and hand

he will press on before the earth, pursued
by the shadow of his final rest.]

He sees work as the only real source of nobility and dignity in life,
and the only honourable basis of society ;

Nadie merece ser dueño
de hacienda que no cultiva,
en carne y en alma viva
con noble intención y empeño.

[No one deserves to be master
of an estate he doesn't cultivate,
in flesh and in living soul
with noble will and desire.]

His is not the poetry of political argument and polemical debate.
Instead, his poetic landscape is peopled with miners, woodcutters,
reapers, farm-hands and, of course, shepherds, all engaged in strenu-
ous physical toil.

Hernández was not the spokesman of the urban proletariat. Far
from it. He urged his fellow labourers to return to the land and leave
behind the corruption of the modern city. For example in this prose
piece of 1934, 'Momento campesino':

Venid conmigo, hermanos; entre estos aires
puros de almendras florecidas nos iremos
robusteciendo huellas y sus analogías en paz.

[Come with me, brothers. Let us go
among the pure airs of the blossoming almond trees
strong in fragrances and their analogies in peace.]

Nonetheless he did not idealize the peasant's lifestyle: he knew only
too well its hardships from his own first hand experience.

Although it was long believed that the two people who were re-
sponsible for the stimulation of Hernández's literary and intellectual
development were Don Luis Almarcha, the canon of the Cathedral

of Orihuela, and José Marín Gutiérrez who wrote under the pseud-
onym of Ramón Sijé, this has now been disproved in a recent book
by José Luis Ferris, *Miguel Hernández: Pasiones, cárcel y muerte de un
poeta* (Madrid, 2002).

While it is true that Don Luis Almarcha, who was a neighbor of
the Hernández family, took a special interest in the young Miguel,
lending him books and directing his reading, and while it is also
true that Sijé exercised a decisive influence on the young Hernández,
it was in fact very much the encouragement and companionship of
Carlos Fenoll and the Fenoll family that forwarded Hernández's lit-
erary ambitions and career.

Carlos and his brother Efrén were the sons of the local baker
who himself dabbled in writing. These constituted a small literary
coterie that met in the Fenoll bakery in *Calle de Arriba* in Orihuela.
The discussions among them were not only literary but political.
Spain was in political crisis. Things had to change. But what should
these changes be? Sijé, although he was not a regular at these bakery
meetings and recitals, had some intellectual input into the group's
thinking. As a sincere Catholic and humane personality, he argued
for something like a Christian democracy. At this stage of his life,
Hernández would not have got much further than this. What would
stay with him for life, however, was the influence of Sijé's deep hu-
manity.

Hernández read avidly the works of San Juan de la Cruz, Gabriel
Miró, Verlaine and Virgil. After these he read the classics of the *Siglo
de Oro*: Cervantes, Lope de Vega, Góngora and Garcilaso. He also
read the moderns, most importantly Antonio Machado and Juan
Ramón Jiménez.

By the time Hernández took the train for Madrid at the begin-
ning of December 1931, he had already established himself as a poet
in provincial Orihuela. He went up to the capital with high hopes of
achieving literary success. But with no money and unable to find em-
ployment, he was back in Orihuela in May 1932. On his way home
Hernández was apprehended for having an invalid ticket, taken off
the train and handed over to the Guardia Civil who treated him
roughly and locked him in prison from Sunday morning until Mon-
day afternoon when they established his identity. Then they threw
him, hungry and penniless, out on the street. Sijé once more came

to his rescue. But the whole experience was not lost on Hernández. It was an unpleasant brush with autocratic authority, the kind of experience that the Peruvian poet César Vallejo was to experience at an impressionable period of his life.

Hernández was still a Catholic, still a believer in that faith instilled in him by his Jesuit teachers, supported by Spanish popular belief at the time, and still influenced by the fervent Catholicism of his friend Sijé. Hernández's friendship with Pablo Neruda dates from 1935. As Sijé was a fervent Catholic, Neruda was an equally fervent Marxist and atheist. And he was unapologetically political in his poetry. Neruda initiated Hernández in the writing of politically committed poetry and liberated him from traditional poetic conventions. It is arguable whether Neruda's influence on Hernández was as radical as the earlier influence of Sijé. Whatever one decides, it was a profound influence.

Hernández spent much time with Neruda and his followers when he travelled to Madrid again in 1934. Eventually, persuaded by their arguments and still as committed as ever to the quest for social justice, he decided to align himself with Neruda's political grouping. He would not continue to be complacent in the face of social inequality nor would he accept the abject poverty in which the average Spanish peasant subsisted. He wanted revolution and the complete restructuring of the existing archaic social order:

> *Libres, campesinos: ¡sed libres! Como las cometas, bajo la dictadura de los niños, encadenadas libremente a un hilo. Libres, campesinos, ¡id! libres, por el libre albedrío de la senda, la voluntad en sujeción, obedeciendo al polvo, a nada, a Dios.*

> [Free, peasants. Be free. Like the kites, under the dictatorship of children, freely bound to a thread. Free, peasants. Go, free, through the volition of the path, the will in subjection, obeying the dust, nothing, God.]

In 1937 he joined the Fifth Regiment as Cultural Commissar and began work on the Andalusian front. He also actively participated in the Second International Congress of Intellectuals in Madrid and Valencia which was attended by André Malraux, Tristan Tzara, Stephen Spender, Ehrenburg and others. In 1937 he also visited the USSR where he went to attend the Fifth Festival of Soviet Theatre. All of these political happenings had their input into *Viento del pueblo* which appeared in the same year. During the Civil War some of his poems were printed by the Republican troops and distributed by them. Hernández found himself writing directly to and for the people.

———

Although he was passionately committed to the Republican cause, Hernández's poetry of the time was not transformed into dull propaganda and he did not write under the guidance of any Communist Party officials. His poetry was heartfelt and written with an obvious compassion and understanding that stretched far beyond the limits of a standard political rallying cry. Yet he was wont at times to issue a powerful and emotive call to arms, as in his poem 'Llamo a la juventud':

> *La juventud siempre empuja,*
> *la juventud siempre vence,*
> *y la salvación de España,*
> *de su juventud depende.*

> [Youth always pushes,
> youth always conquers,
> and the salvation of Spain
> depends on its youth.]

The title of his collection of poems publis
Pueblo, conjures up the image of a hurrica
the entire nation and propelling it towards i
ist political views find expression in such po
ternacional caído en España' ('To the Internat
Spain'), 'Ceniciento Mussolini' ('Ashen Muss
España' ('Peasant of Spain'), the very titles of
doubt as to their political nature. The first po
'Elegía primera' ('First Elegy'), deals with the
poet, Federico García Lorca, a crime which touc
Spanish artist and liberal. In the poem, dedica

poet, Hernández details the loss suffered by the Spanish nation on losing its most talented literary genius:

> *Muere un poeta y la creación se siente*
> *herida y moribunda en las entrañas.*

> [A poet dies and creation feels
> wounded and sick-to-death in its innards.]

In the terminology of a more innocent age, Hernández was a true brother of the people. He shared their roots and experienced first hand many of the hardships they were forced to endure. He was no theorizing intellectual, preaching to the masses from the comfort and safety of middle class surroundings. As he himself declared:

> *Hambrientamente lucho yo, con todas mis brechas,*
> *cicatrices y heridas, señales y recuerdos del hambre,*
> *contra tantas barrigas satisfechas:*
> *cerdos con un origen peor que el de los cerdos.*

> [Hungrily I fight, with all my gashes,
> scars and wounds, marks and memories
> of hunger, against so many stuffed bellies:
> pigs of worse gin than pigs.]

tions of the enemy, so graphically expressed, hout Hernández's work of the period. In 'El oung Ploughboy') he launches an attack on exploitative land-owners when he paints a oung boy ploughing in the fields and being by this heavy and gruelling work for which ore than a pittance:

> *iatura,*
> *us pies*
> *ura.*

[Each day he is
more root, less child,
hearing the voice of the tomb
beneath his feet.]

His second collection of poems written during the war, *El hombre acecha* (*Man In Ambush*) describes the violence and loss of life incurred during the Spanish Civil War and it also contains a message of renewed defiance. In poems like 'El herido' ('The Wounded') and 'El tren de los heridos' ('The Train of The Wounded') Hernández depicts the human suffering which a prolonged civil war inevitably entails. These poems are soaked in the blood of the fallen heroes of the Republican army:

El tren lluvioso de la sangre suelta,
el frágil tren de los que se desangran,
el silencioso, el doloroso, el pálido,
el tren callado de los sufrimientos.

Silencio.
....

Van derramando piernas, brazos, ojos,
van arrojando por el tren pedazos.
Pasan dejando rastros de amargura,
otra vía láctea de estelares miembros.

Silencio.

[The train drenched in bold blood,
the fragile train of those who bleed,
the silent, the painful, the pale,
the noiseless train of the suffering.

Silence.
....

Spilling legs, arms, eyes, they go,
hurling pieces along the train they pass.

They pass leaving traces of bitterness,
another milky track of stellar limbs.

Silence.]

In *Pueblo*, Hernández proclaims the impotence of modern mili-
tary technology in the face of human solidarity. Machine guns and
aeroplanes are no match for man's own *hueso* ('bone') and his *diez
dedos* ('ten fingers'). In poems such as 'Rusia' and 'La fábrica ciudad'
he adapts his own familiar vocabulary of *manzanas* ('apples'), *trigo*
('wheat') and *ganaderías* ('livestock') to his new subject matter. The
final poem, 'Canción última' ('Final Song') ends the book on a note
of optimism. There is hope for a better future and a Spain that is
strong, hard-working, peaceful and free:

*El odio se amortigua
detrás de la ventana.
Será la garra suave.
Dejadme la esperanza.*

[Hatred is soothed
behind the window.
The paw will be gentle.
Leave me hope.]

At the end of the Civil War Hernández was arrested as he tried to
make his escape into Portugal. He was jailed in the prison of Huelva,
then in Seville and then in Madrid. Other prisons followed until he
was finally incarcerated in Alicante. He died on March 28, 1942,
primarily of tuberculosis.

THE PRISON POEMS

In the course of his terrible years in prison Hernández pondered the
circumstances of his life and experiences, past and present. The re-
sults of this are to be found in *Cancionero y romancero de ausencias*.
In this book there are lyrics of terrible anguish. There are many
poems expressing the sorrow he feels because of his forced separation
from his wife Josefina:

No puedo olvidar
que no tengo alas,
que no tengo mar,
vereda ni nada
con que irte a besar.

[I cannot forget
that I have no wings,
that I have no sea
no path or anything
to go and kiss you.]

There are also poems about the loss of his dead child:

Muerto niño, muerto mío:
nadie nos siente en la tierra
donde haces caliente el frío.

[Dead child, my dead child.
No one feels us in the earth
where you make the cold warm.]

And there are poems about his dead comrades-in-arms and the misery of his imprisonment. But there are no regrets. There is no nihilistic disillusionment. His humanity survives, battered but triumphant. There is a deep compassion for suffering humanity and a positive assertion of human dignity.

Perhaps the most famous of Hernández's poems is his 'Nanas de la cebolla'. It is appropriately written in popular form which powerfully conveys the earthiness of its subject matter. At the same time it possesses a technical sophistication that is needed to express the complex emotions that he wants to articulate. The deeply human situation out of which the poem arose was a letter from Hernández's wife Josefina telling the poet (who was in prison at the time) that she had nothing but bread and onion to feed their child. Instead of responding with self-pity or resentment, as one might expect, the poet bursts into a celebration of love and life. Human life, specifically human love, has the capacity to transcend poverty, to transcend hunger, which is nonetheless frankly confronted:

> *Hambre y cebolla:*
> *hielo negro y escarcha*
> *grande y redonda.*

> [Hunger and onion:
> black ice and hoarfrost
> large and round.]

Images of birds are employed to represent the soaring of the human spirit above physical deprivation; *'Alondra de mi casa,/ ríete mucho'* ['Lark of my house/ laugh with delight']; *'¡Cuánto jilguero/ se remonta, aletea,/ desde su cuerpo'* ['How many linnets/ soar and flutter/ off your body']. For the poet, just to think of his child alive is enough to raise his spirit. Life, even without the niceties of good food, is amazingly precious. With a stoicism born of profound suffering, Hernández concludes:

> *No te derrumbes.*
> *No sepas lo que pasa*
> *ni lo que ocurre.*

> [Don't fall.
> Ignore what happens
> or what goes on.]

Although so different in its images and techniques, Hernández's 'Nanas de la cebolla' exults in the same joy of life as Dylan Thomas's 'Out of the Sighs':

> Out of the sighs a little comes,
> But not of grief, for I have knocked down that
> Before the agony; the spirit grows,
> Forgets, and cries;
> A little comes, is tasted and found good.

There is one special poem among Hernández's last poems, 'Después del amor' ('After Love'), from *Cancionero y romancero de ausencias*, which in some way embodies this man of high idealism, deep humanity and terrible suffering. Prison and the Civil War resonate ominously through the poem:

> *Piedras, hombres como piedras,*
> *duros y plenos de encono,*
> *chocan en el aire, donde*
> *chocan las piedras de pronto.*
>
> ....
>
> *Cuerpos como un mar voraz,*
> *entrechocado, furioso.*
> *Solitariamente atados*
> *por el amor, por el odio,*
> *por las venas surgen hombres,*
> *cruzan las ciudades, torvos.*

> [Stones, men like stones,
> hard and full of rancour,
> clash in the air where
> suddenly stones clash
>
> ....
>
> Bodies like a greedy sea
> clashing in fury.
> In solitude bound
> by love, by hatred.
> Men rise out of all veins;
> spiteful they cross cities.]

Confronting the terrible realities he has been through, unrelenting even now as he lingers sick in prison, Hernández's spirit remains unvanquished. There is one voice he hears that still can manage to support him:

> *Sólo una voz, a lo lejos,*
> *siempre a lo lejos la oigo,*

acompaña y hace ir
igual que el cuello a los hombros.

Sólo una voz me arrebata
este armazón espinoso
de vello retrocedido
y erizado que me pongo.

Los secos vientos no pueden
secar los mares jugosos.
Y el corazón permanece
fresco en su cárcel de agosto
porque esa voz es el arma
más tierna de los arroyos.

[Alone, in the distance, a voice
I hear ever distant.
It attends and compels
as the neck the shoulder.

Just one voice strips me
of this prickly hide
of raised and bristling
hair that I display.

Dry winds will not
parch the oozy seas.
And the heart stays fresh
in its August gaol
under the voice's spell,
gentlest way of streams.]

The love which Hernández ever felt for his fellow human beings, for his wife and family, for his friends, for the world of nature... that deep abiding love stayed with the poet to the end, saving him from the devouring bitterness of cynicism, disillusionment and resentment. Here is the conclusion of 'Después del amor':

Amor: aleja mi ser
de sus primeros escombros,
y edificándome, dicta
una verdad como un soplo.

[Love, save me from
my former ruin,
and building me back, utter
some breathlike truth.]

It is generally agreed, I think it fair to say, that, at least in modern times, poetry and ideological politics have not been good for one another. The early Auden is a classic warning. Brecht is sometimes considered a rare exception. And sometimes Mayakovsky or even Blok. It may be that the generalizations essential to political thought and emotion run counter to the concrete specificity demanded of modern poetry. Or it may be that politics usurps the aesthetic concerns essential to the creation of art. At any rate, Hernández's poetic example is of extraordinary value in demonstrating the tension that almost invariably exists between poetry and politics. It is true that he wrote patently political poetry and that for a time he put his art at the service of a political cause. But it is equally true that in his last great collection *Cancionero y romancero de ausencias* Hernandez's art is placed at the service of a humanity that ultimately transcends the concerns of historical politics. It is best described as a poetry of the human spirit, however one describes that entity. But it is not a poetry that cynically abandons political concerns; rather, it humanizes them. For that reason it seems to me that it will survive and grow in stature.

Finally, perhaps the real key to the overall mood of Hernández's *Prison Poems* is to be found in Segismundo's famous speech in Calderón's *La vida es sueño* in which there is the ultimate cry of release from the suffering of the human condition, the protest against an uncomprehending fate (in the Spanish-speaking world, this speech is as famous as Hamlet's 'To be or not to be ...'):

As you treat me so,
Heaven, I try to understand

what was my crime against you
by being born, while still
I grasp by the very fact
of birth what crime it was.
Your unrelenting justice
has sufficient cause:
Man's greatest crime
is simply to have been born.

This I'd only know
to expend all my cares
(aside, Heaven, from birth itself):
What more offence can I
inflict on you to justify
your further punishment?
Were other men not born?
That being so, what blessings
have they had
that never have been mine?

The bird is born plumaged
in perfect beauty.
Scarcely a feathered bloom,
a winged bouquet,
it cleaves the vaulted heaven
and leaves behind, becalmed,
its haven nest.
Then how is it that I
who have more soul
enjoy less liberty?

The beast is born
with skin of dappled beauty.
No sooner constellation
by Nature's skilful brush,
when sheer necessity, unremitting
and cruel, teaches it cruelty,
a monster in its labyrinth.
Then how is it that I,

endowed with better instinct,
enjoy less liberty?

The fish, that draws no breath,
is born, a freak of spawn and slime.
A ship of scales, no sooner
sighted on the waves,
it spins through every quarter,
sounding the immense
coldness of the depths.
Then how is it that I
who have more free will
enjoy less liberty?

The stream is born, a snake
uncoiling in the flowers.
This silver serpent scarcely
breaks through blossoms
but it celebrates their grace
with music, flowing with majesty
to the open plain.
Then how can I
who have greater life
enjoy less liberty?

Hitting this pitch of grief,
a volcano, an Etna,
I'd tear from out my breast
pieces of my heart.
What law, justice, reason,
can deny to man
a privilege so sweet, so tall a grace,
as God gives stream,
fish, beast and bird?

(Tr. Michael Smith)

Note on Hernández's Imprisonment

The events surrounding Hernández's imprisonment and death are important, especially as they constitute the background of most of the poems in *Cancionero*. The following is a summary of what is known to have taken place. For the information contained in the summary, I am indebted to Augustín Sánchez Vidal (*Obra Completa, I*, Espasa Calpe, Madrid, 1993).

With the military collapse of the Republic in 1939, Hernández sought out the help of whatever friends of his he could contact. For one reason or another he was unsuccessful in getting the help he needed. He then attempted to cross the Spanish/Portuguese border at Rosal de la Frontera. However, he was quickly arrested by the Portuguese police who handed him over to the Spanish authorities. He was then moved to Madrid where he was held in the prison of Torrijos. From that prison he was released, and it is conjectured that this happened simply through a bureaucratic bungle. Against the strenuous advice of his friends, Hernández made his way back to Orihuela, back to Josefina and his family. There, as everyone except himself anticipated, he was re-arrested and imprisoned in the Madrid prison of Conde de Toreno. Conditions in that prison were appalling. More than half of the prisoners there were condemned to death and the majority of these were shot within six months. It is thought that Hernández survived this fate because the Nationalist State did not want a repeat of the international scandal that followed the murder of Lorca.

From Madrid, Hernández was then moved to the provincial prison of Palencia where conditions were as bad, if not worse than those in Conde de Toreno. His health began to deteriorate seriously. In 1940, he was moved again , this time to the prison in Ocaña after a period in the prison of Yeserías. Finally, on June 28, 1941, he was incarcerated in the Reformatorio de Adultos in Alicante where at least he could receive visits from his family with the exception of his father who refused to see the son who had disgraced him in the eyes of conservative Orihuela.

The pneumonia he had contracted in Palencia and the bronchitis contracted in Ocaña developed into tuberculosis. The prison authorities were aware of his condition and also knew that there was the possibility of a cure by transferring him to the anti-tubercular clinic of Porta Coeli in Valencia. It is still unclear why permission for this transfer was delayed until days before his death. The suggestion of one Hernándian biographer, Ramón Pérez Álvarez, is that the prison chaplains, in particular Father Vendrell, demanded that he and Josefina go through a religious marriage (Miguel and Josefina had married in a civil ceremony). In order to secure Josefina's legal status as his wife after his death, Hernández, actively encouraged by his old friend Don Luis Almarcha, reluctantly went through a religious marriage. Almarcha was a very influential figure at this time, and Pérez Álvarez is of the opinion that he did not do all he could have done to save his one-time protégé; that once Don Luis Almarcha had seen Hernández married in the eyes of the Church, he lost interest in his case: his soul was saved, so what did it matter whether he died in prison or outside it. This assessment has been denied on the basis that it exaggerates the influence of Almarcha. The mystery remains.

On March 27, Josefina visited Hernández for the last time. She knew he was dying. On the following day, March 28, the poet was dead.

NOTE ON THIS VERSION OF THE PRISON POEMS

The text of *Cancionero y romancero de ausencias* (literally *Songbook and Ballad Book of Absences*, which I have titled *The Prison Poems*), is fraught with textual difficulties, way beyond my competence to deal with. Hernández did not live to put the book together. The notebook in which most of the poems were written, though not all, was passed on to Hernández's widow, Josefina Manresa. The poems were written (so far as I can gather) between 1937 and 1939. After Hernández's death, Josefina attempted to get various publishers to undertake the publication of his work. But there were delays and problems. In the face of all this, I have opted to go along with the latest, and it seems to me, the most competent editors. Perhaps the title *The Prison Poems* is a bit misleading, but I think not. Most of the poems have the prison background.

The language of *The Prison Poems* is tough and tortuous. It combines the Spanish baroque with surrealism. There is a good deal of awkwardness which doubtless would have been eliminated had Hernández been working in better conditions and had lived to revise his work. That said, Hernández's Spanish has a powerful muscularity that is entirely appropriate to the experiences that constitute the material of *The Prison Poems*. He never aspired to the sophisticated polish of Lorca. Equally, he avoids the often facile fluidity of Neruda. Although his poetry cannot be said to be as experimental as that of Vallejo, it possesses the Peruvian's rock-solid integrity of purpose. I have attempted to be true to that integrity even at the cost of awkward English in some places.

Acknowledgements and Select Bibliography

My single greatest debt in the undertaking and completing of this version of *The Prison Poems* I owe to my good friend, Luis Huerga. It is no polite exaggeration to say that without his assistance this version would simply not exist. Having said that, however, I must dissociate him from whatever errors or stylistic lapses the reader may come upon. I must also thank my daughter Alice for her generous help with the writing of the introductory material.

Finally I must thank my friend, Luis Ingelmo, for all the work he has done on this translation.

Because they are answerable to an already existing original, accessible to anyone who can read the language of the original, translators are vulnerable in a way that most other literary workers are not; and in the translation of difficult poetry, that vulnerability increases a hundredfold. Hispanists are entitled and obliged to call the translator to book for errors committed, but they should bear in mind that this work of translation was done primarily for those who do not have access to the originals.

Books and articles on Hernández and his work are now numerous. The following are simply the books I needed for what I set out to do.

1.   Miguel Hernández, *Obra Completa, I* and *II*. Edición crítica de Augustín Sánchez Vidal y José Rovira con la colaboración de

Carmen Alemany (Madrid, 1992). This is the definitive critical text on which the present translation is based.

2. Ramos, V., *Miguel Hernández* (Madrid, 1973).

3. Cano Ballesta, J., *La Poesía de Miguel Hernández* (Madrid, 1962).

4. Manresa, Josefina, *Recuerdos de la Viuda de Miguel Hernández* (Madrid, 1980).

5. Ferris, José Luis, *Miguel Hernández: Pasiones, cárcel y muerte de un poeta* (Madrid, 2002).

This translation is dedicated to my wife, Irene, without whose constant encouragement throughout many years it would never have been done or published.

The Prison Poems

A

CANCIONERO Y ROMANCERO DE AUSENCIAS

1

Ropas con su olor.
paños con su aroma.
Se alejó en su cuerpo,
me dejó en sus ropas.
Lecho sin calor,
sábana de sombra.
Se ausentó en su cuerpo.
Se quedó en sus ropas.

2

Negros ojos negros.
El mundo se abría
sobre tus pestañas
de negras distancias.
Dorada mirada.
El mundo se cierra
sobre tus pestañas
lluviosas y negras.

A

SONGBOOK AND BALLADBOOK
OF ABSENCES

1

Clothes that keep her scent,
linen that holds her fragrance.
She went away in body,
in her clothes she stayed with me.
Bed without warmth,
sheet of shadow.
She went away in body;
in her clothes, remained.

2

Black, black eyes.
The world opened
upon your eyelashes
darkened by distance.
Gold-like gaze.
The world closes
upon your eyelashes
dark and gloomy.

3

No quiso ser.

No conoció el encuentro
del hombre y la mujer.
El amoroso vello
no pudo florecer.
Detuvo sus sentidos
negándose a saber
y descendieron diáfanos
ante el amanecer.
Vio turbio su mañana
y se quedó en su ayer.

No quiso ser.

4

Tus ojos parecen
agua removida.
¿Qué son?

Tus ojos parecen
el agua más turbia
de tu corazón.
¿Qué fueron? ¿Qué son?

5

En el fondo del hombre
agua removida.

En el agua más clara
quiero ver la vida.

En el fondo del hombre
agua removida.

3

He would not be.

He never knew
how man and woman meet.
In him love's down
did not come to bloom.
His senses all held back
admitting no knowledge
and still transparent
sank from sight at dawn.
He saw a blurred tomorrow
and so he clung to yesterday.

He would not be.

4

Your eyes
like disturbed water.
What can they be?

Your eyes
like darkest water
from your heart.
What have they been? What are they?

5

In the depths of man,
troubled water.

In the clearest water,
I seem to see life.

In the depths of man,
troubled water.

En el agua más clara
sombra sin salida.

En el fondo del hombre
agua removida.

6

El cementerio está cerca
de donde tú y yo dormimos,
entre nopales azules,
pitas azules y niños
que gritan vívidamente
si un muerto nubla el camino.
De aquí al cementerio, todo
es azul, dorado, límpido.
Cuatro pasos, y los muertos.
Cuatro pasos, y los vivos.
Límpido, azul y dorado,
se hace allí remoto el hijo.

7

Sangre remota.
Remoto cuerpo,
dentro de todo:
dentro, muy dentro
de mis pasiones,
de mis deseos.

8

¿Qué quiere el viento de encono
que baja por el barranco
y violenta las ventanas
mientras te visto de abrazos?

Derribarnos, arrastrarnos.

In the clearest water,
entrapped shadow.

In the depths of man,
troubled water.

6

The cemetery is nearby
where you and I sleep,
among blue prickly pear,
blue agaves and children
who shout vociferously
if a death darkens the road.
From here to the cemetery, all
is blue, golden, limpid.
Four paces, and the dead.
Four paces, and the living.
Limpid, blue, golden, there
my son becomes remote.

7

Remote blood.
Remote body,
inside all things.
Inside, deep inside
my passions,
my desires.

8

What ails the plagued wind?
Down the gorge it blows
and blasts in our windows
as my embraces clothe you.

It would lay us low, drag us along.

Derribadas, arrastradas,
las dos sangres se alejaron.
¿Qué sigue queriendo el viento
cada vez más enconado?

Separarnos.

9

VALS DE LOS ENAMORADOS Y UNIDOS HASTE SIEMPRE

No salieron jamás
del vergel del abrazo.
Y ante el rojo rosal
de los besos rodaron.

Huracanes quisieron
con rencor separarlos.
Y las hachas tajantes
y los rígidos rayos.

Aumentaron la tierra
de las pálidas manos.
Precipicios midieron,
por el viento impulsados
entre bocas deshechas.
Recorrieron naufragios,
cada vez más profundos
en sus cuerpos, sus brazos.
Perseguidos, hundidos
por un gran desamparo
de recuerdos y lunas,
de noviembres y marzos,
aventados se vieron
como polvo liviano:
aventados se vieron,
pero siempre abrazados.

Dragged along, battered down,
our two bloods moved away.
Still the wind's anger mounts:
what has it in mind?

To separate us.

9

WALTZ OF THE LOVERS UNITED FOREVER

They never left
the orchard of embrace,
and they rolled
by the red rosebush of kisses.

Spiteful whirlwinds,
sharp axes,
stiff lightning,
strove to part them.

They spread
their pale earthy hands.
Swept off by the wind,
amid gashed mouths,
they spanned chasms.
They went through ever more
perilous shipwrecks
in their bodies, their arms.
Harassed, sunk
by a great desertion
of memories and moons,
of Novembers and Marches,
they saw themselves driven
like fickle dust:
they saw themselves driven,
but always embraced.

10

Un viento ceniciento
clama en la habitación
donde clamaba ella
ciñéndose a mi voz.

Cámara solitaria,
con el herido son
del ceniciento viento
clamante alrededor.

Espejo despoblado.
Despavorido arcón
frente al retrato árido
y al lecho sin calor.

Cenizas que alborota
el viento que no amó.

En medio de la noche,
la cenicienta cámara
con viento y sin amores.

11

Como la higuera joven
de los barrancos eras.
Y cuando yo pasaba
sonabas en la sierra.
Como la higuera joven,
resplandeciente y ciega.

Como la higuera eres.
Como la higuera vieja.
Y paso, y me saludan
silencio y hojas secas.

Como la higuera eres
que el rayo envejeciera.

10

An ashen wind
moans in the room
where her moaning
clung to my voice.

Desolate chamber
with the wounded sound
of the ashen wind
moaning around.

Deserted mirror,
inert chest
before the arid portrait
and the bed robbed of warmth.

Ashes stirred
by the wind she did not love.

In the dead of night
the ashen chamber
windy and loveless.

11

You were like the young
fig tree of the ravines.
In the sierra you rustled
as I went by.
Like the young fig tree
resplendent and blind.

You are like the fig tree.
Like the old fig tree.
And I go by greeted
by hush and dry leaves.

You are like the fig tree
that aged when lightning struck.

12

El sol, la rosa y el niño
flores de un día nacieron.
Los de cada día son
soles, flores, niños nuevos.

Mañana no seré yo:
otro será el verdadero.
Y no seré más allá
de quien quiera su recuerdo.

Flor de un día es lo más grande
al pie de lo más pequeño.
Flor de la luz el relámpago,
y flor del instante el tiempo.

Entre las flores te fuiste.
Entre las flores me quedo.

13

Besarse, mujer,
al sol, es besarnos
en toda la vida.
Ascienden los labios
eléctricamente
vibrantes de rayos,
con todo el furor
de un sol entre cuatro.
Besarse a la luna,
mujer, es besarnos
en toda la muerte.
Descienden los labios,
con toda la luna,
pidiendo su ocaso,
del labio de arriba,
del labio de abajo,
gastada y helada
y en cuatro pedazos.

12

The sun, the rose, the child,
sprang up as one day's flowers.
Those of every day
are new suns, flowers, children.

Tomorrow I won't be myself:
my true self will be another.
I shall be no more
than the memory of any who care.

Next to the smallest, the greatest
thing is one day's flower.
The flower of light is lightning;
the instant's flower is time.

Among flowers, you left.
Among flowers, I stay.

13

To kiss in the sunlight,
woman, is to kiss
all of life.
The lips rise
electrically,
a frizzle of bolts,
with the full flare
of one sun in four.
To kiss in the moonlight,
woman, is to kiss
all of death.
The lips descend
with all of the full moon:
seeking the setting,
of the upper lip,
of the nether lip,
spent and icy
a moon in four bits.

14

Llegó tan hondo el beso
que traspasó y emocionó los muertos.

El beso trajo un brío
que arrebató la boca de los vivos.

El hondo beso grande
sintió breves los labios al ahondarse.

El beso aquel que quiso
cavar los muertos y sembrar los vivos.

15

Si te perdiera...
Si te encontrara
bajo la tierra.

Bajo la tierra
del cuerpo mío,
siempre sedienta.

16

Cuerpo del amanecer:
flor de la carne florida.
Siento que no quiso ser
más allá de flor tu vida.
Corazón que en el tamaño
de un día se abre y se cierra.
La flor nunca cumple un año,
y lo cumple bajo tierra.

14

The kiss plunged so deeply
it pierced and moved the dead.

The kiss brought a force
that seized all living mouths.

The great deep kiss,
on intensifying, felt scant lips.

That one kiss that would
dig over the dead and sow the living.

15

If I should lose you ...
If I should find you
under the earth.

Under my body's
ever thirsting
earth.

16

Dawning body:
flower of burgeoning flesh.
I feel your life's refusal
to be more than flower.
Heart that is opened and closed
in the span of a single day.
Flower that never outlasts a year
but under the earth.

17

En este campo
estuvo el mar.
Alguna vez volverá.
Si alguna vez una gota
roza este campo, este campo
siente el recuerdo del mar.
Alguna vez volverá.

18

Cada vez que paso
bajo tu ventana,
me azota el aroma
que aún flota en tu casa.
Cada vez que paso
junto al cementerio
me arrastra la fuerza
que aún sopla en tus huesos.

19

El corazón es agua
que se acaricia y canta.

El corazón es puerta
que se abre y se cierra.

El corazón es agua
que se remueve, arrolla,
se arremolina, mata.

17

The sea once covered
this field.
It's sure to return.
If but a drop grazes
this field, this field
yearns for the sea.
It's sure to return.

18

Each time I walk
past your window
the scent still there
will buffet me.
Each time I walk
past the cemetery
I am drawn by the force
your bones still breathe.

19

The heart is water
that is stroked and sings.

The heart is a gate
that opens and shuts.

The heart is water
that stirs, drags,
swirls, kills.

20

Tierra. La despedida
siempre es una agonía.

Ayer nos despedimos.
Ayer agonizamos.
Tierra en medio.
Hoy morimos.

21

Por eso las estaciones
saben a muerte, y los puertos.
Por eso cuando partimos
se deshojan los pañuelos.

Cadáveres vivos somos
en el horizonte, lejos.

22

Cada vez más presente.
Como si un rayo raudo
te trajera a mi pecho.
Como un lento, rayo
lento.

Cada vez más ausente.
Como si un tren lejano
recorriera mi cuerpo.
Como si un negro barco
negro.

20

Earth. Parting
is always agonizing.

Yesterday we parted,
yesterday we suffered death-throes.
Earth is between.
Today we die.

21

So that's why stations
and wharves taste of death.
So that's why on parting
handkerchiefs unleaf.

We are living corpses
faraway on the horizon.

22

Ever more present.
As if a swift shaft
brought you to my chest.
Like a slow
slow shaft.

Ever more absent.
As if a distant train
went through my body.
As if a black
black ship.

23

Si nosotros viviéramos
lo que la rosa, con su intensidad,
el profundo perfume de los cuerpos
sería mucho más.

¡Ay, breve vida intensa
de un día de rosales secular
pasaste por la casa
igual, igual, igual
que un meteoro herido, perfumado
de hermosura y verdad.

La huella que has dejado es un abismo
con ruinas de rosal
donde un perfume que no cesa hace
que vayan nuestros cuerpos más allá.

24

Una fotografía.
Un cartón expresivo,
envuelto por los meses
en los rincones íntimos.

Un agua de distancia
quiero beber: gozar
un fondo de fantasma.

Un cartón me conmueve.
Un cartón me acompaña.

23

If ours were the rose's
span of life, alike intense,
our bodies' fragrance
would reach far greater depth.

Ah, intense brief life
of rosebush age,
you went through the house
the same, same, same
as a meteor hurt and perfumed
with beauty and truth.

You left an abysmal hollow
all rosebush wreck,
your body and mine
goaded on by ceaseless perfume.

24

A photograph.
A telling piece of cardboard
the months have left
in inner nooks.

Let me drink
a distant water, delight
in ghost depth.

Cardboard that moves me.
Cardboard that keeps me company.

25

Llegó con tres heridas:
la del amor,
la de la muerte,
la de la vida.

Con tres heridas viene:
la de la vida,
la del amor,
la de la muerte.

Con tres heridas yo:
la de la vida,
la de la muerte,
la del amor.

26

Escribí en el arenal
los tres nombres de la vida:
vida, muerte, amor.
Una ráfaga de mar,
tantas claras veces ida,
vino y nos borró.

27

Cogedme, cogedme.
Dejadme, dejadme,
fieras, hombres, sombras,
soles, flores, mares.
Cogedme.
Dejadme.

25

He arrived with three wounds:
that of love,
that of death,
that of life.

With three wounds he comes:
that of life,
that of love,
that of death.

With three wounds, I:
that of life,
that of death,
that of love.

26

I wrote on the sands
the three names of life:
life, death, love.
A sea wave
that had often passed clear
came and wiped us out.

27

Take me, take me.
Leave me, leave me.
Wild beasts, men, shadows,
suns, flowers, seas.
Take me.
Leave me.

28

Tus ojos se me van
de mis ojos, y vuelven
después de recorrer
un páramo de ausentes.
Tus brazos se desploman
en mis brazos y ascienden
retrocediendo ante esa
desolación que sientes.
Desolación con hielo,
aún mi calor te vence.

29

Ausencia en todo veo:
tus ojos la reflejan.
Ausencia en todo escucho:
tu voz a tiempo suena.
Ausencia en todo aspira:
tu aliento huele a hierba.
Ausencia en todo toco:
tu cuerpo se despuebla.
Ausencia en todo pruebo:
tu boca me destierra.
Ausencia en todo siento:
ausencia, ausencia, ausencia.

28

Your eyes see out
from mine and return
when they've crossed
a moor of parted ones.
Your arms collapse
in mine and rise
to retreat in face
of that despair in you.
Icy despair,
even my heat conquers you.

29

I see absence in all things:
your eyes mirror it.
I hear absence in all things:
your voice keeps pace with it.
I breathe absence in all things:
your breath smells of grass.
I touch absence in all things:
your body is deserted.
I taste absence in all things:
Your mouth banishes me.
I feel absence in all things.
Absence. Absence. Absence.

30

¿De qué adoleció
la mujer aquélla?

Del mal peor:
del mal de la ausencias.

Y el hombre aquél.

¿De qué murió
la mujer aquélla?

Del mal peor:
del mal de las ausencias.

Y el hombre aquél.

31

Tan cercanos, y a veces
qué lejos los sentimos,
tú yéndote a los muertos,
yo yéndome a los vivos.

32

Tú eres fatal ante le muerte.
Yo soy fatal ante la vida.
Yo siempre en pie quisiera verte,
tú quieres verte siempre hundida.

30

What ill besets
that woman?

The worst of ills:
the ill of absence.

And that man, too.

What brought death
on that woman?

The worst of ills:
the ill of absence.

And that man, too.

31

So close, yet sometimes
how far apart we feel:
you on the way to the dead,
I on the way to the living.

32

You are fated to death.
I am fated to life.
I wish you always stood erect.
You only think of being crushed.

33

Llevadme al cementerio
de los zapatos viejos.

Echadme a todas horas
la pluma de la escoba.

Sembradme con estatuas
de rígida mirada.

Por un huerto de bocas,
futuras y doradas,
relumbrará mi sombra.

34

La luciérnaga en celo
relumbra más.

La mujer sin el hombre
apagada va.

Apagado va el hombre
sin luz de mujer.

La luciérnaga en celo
se deja ver.

33

Bring me to the cemetery
of old shoes.

Pelt me at all times
with the hair of brooms.

Sow me among statues
of unyielding gaze.

In an orchard of mouths
impending and golden
my shadow will glimmer.

34

The glowworm in heat
shines the brighter.

Woman without man
goes about lustreless.

Without woman's light
man goes about lustreless.

The while it's in heat
the glowworm is visible.

35

Uvas, granadas, dátiles,
doradas, rojas, rojos,
hierbabuena del alma,
azafrán de los poros.
Uvas como tu frente,
uvas como tus ojos.
Granadas con la herida
de tu florido asombro,
dátiles con tu esbelta
ternura sin retorno,
azafrán, hierbabuena
llueves a grandes chorros
sobre la mesa pobre,
gastada, del otoño,
muerto que te derramas,
muerto que yo conozco,
muerto frutal, caído
con octubre en los hombros.

36

Muerto mío, muerto mío:
nadie nos siente en la tierra
donde haces caliente el frío.

35

Grapes, pomegranates, dates,
golden and red,
the soul's mint,
the pores' saffron.
Grapes like your forehead,
grapes like your eyes.
Pomegranates with the wound
of your wonder's flower.
Dates with your slender
unrelenting gentleness.
Saffron, mint
you rain down in spurts
on autumn's poor
spent table,
dead one that overflows,
dead one I know,
dead fruit tree, fallen
with October on your shoulders.

36

Dead in childhood, my loved one.
No one heeds us in the earth
where you turn cold to warmth.

37

Las gramas, las ortigas
en el otoño avanzan
con una suavidad
y una ternura largas.

El otoño, un sabor
que separa las cosas,
las aleja y arrastra.

Llueve sobre el tejado
como sobre una caja
mientras la hierba crece
como una joven ala.

Las gramas, las ortigas
nutre una misma savia.

38

Atraviesa la calle,
dicen que todo el barrio
y yo digo que nadie.
Pero escuchando, ansiando,
oigo en su mismo centro
el alma de tus pasos,
y me parece un sueño
que, sobre el empedrado,
alza tu pie su íntimo
sonido descansado.

37

The grasses, the nettles
grow further in autumn
in smooth and gentle
lengthiness.

Autumn, a taste
of divisions,
dislodgments and haulings.

It rains on the rooftop
as on a casket
while the grass grows
like a young wing.

A like sap feeds
the grasses, the nettles.

38

It crosses the street,
the whole district, they say;
and I say it's no one.
But listening and yearning
I hear at the core
the steps of your soul,
and I think it's a dream
how that foot of yours
treads on the cobbles
with a step light and dear.

39

Troncos de soledad,
barrancos de tristeza
donde rompo a llorar.

40

Todas las casas son ojos
que resplandecen y acechan.

Todas las casas son bocas
que escupen, muerden y besan.

Todas las casas son brazos
que se empujan y se estrechan.

De todas las casas salen
soplos de sombra y de selva.

En todas hay un clamor
de sangres insatisfechas.

Y a un grito todas las casas
se asaltan y se despueblan.

Y a un grito, todas se aplacan,
y se fecundan, y esperan.

39

Trunks of solitude,
desolate ravines
where I burst into tears.

40

All the houses are eyes
that flash and lurk.

All the houses are mouths
that spit, bite and kiss.

All the houses are arms
pushing, embracing.

From all of the houses blow
gusts of shadow and forest.

In all of them there is a clamour
of unsatisfied blood.

And at a cry all the houses
are stormed and abandoned.

And at a cry all are appeased,
and couple, and hope.

41

El amor ascendía entre nosotros
como la luna entre las dos palmeras
que nunca se abrazaron.

El íntimo rumor de los dos cuerpos
hacia el arrullo un oleaje trajo,
pero la ronca voz fue atenazada,
fueron pétreos los labios.

El ansia de ceñir movió la carne,
esclareció los huesos inflamados,
pero los brazos al querer tenderse
murieron en los brazos.

Pasó el amor, la luna, entre nosotros
y devoró los cuerpos solitarios.
Y somos dos fantasmas que se buscan
y se encuentran lejanos.

42

Cuando paso por tu puerta,
la tarde me viene a herir
con su hermosura desierta
que no acaba de morir.

Tu puerta no tiene casa
ni calle: tiene un camino,
por donde la tarde pasa
como un agua sin destino.

Tu puerta tiene una llave
que para todos rechina.
En la tarde hermosa y grave,
ni una sola golondrina.

41

As the moon between two palm
trees that never intertwined,
love arose between us.

The two bodies' innermost
beat upheaved the cooing;
but the raucous voice was stifled.
Lips became stone.

Longing to embrace urged on the flesh,
fanned burning bones;
but once outstretched, arm died in arm,
their efforts all in vain.

Love, the moon, between us strode,
devoured our lonely bodies.
And we are ghosts that seek
and find each remote from each.

42

When I walk past your door
evening turns to wound me
with its deserted beauty
that will not breathe its last.

Your door has neither house
nor street: it has a road
along which evening rolls
as would unguided water.

Your door has a key
that clicks to one and all.
In the fine, grave evening
there's not a single swallow.

Hierbas en tu puerta crecen
de ser tan poco pisada.
Todas las cosas padecen
sobre la tarde abrasada.

La piel de tu puerta, ¿encierra
un lecho que compartir?
La tarde no encuentra tierra
donde ponerse a morir.

Llena de un siglo de ocasos
de una tarde azul de abierta,
hundo en tu puerta mis pasos
y no sales a tu puerta.

En tu puerta no hay ventana
por donde poderte hablar.
Tarde, hermosura lejana
que nunca pude lograr.

Y la tarde azul corona
tu puerta gris de vacía.
Y la noche se amontona
sin esperanzas de día.

Weeds sprout at your doorway,
so little is it trodden;
all things suffer
in the glowing evening.

Your door's skin, does it hold
a bed one could share?
The evening finds no ground
on which it may expire.

Filled with an age of sunsets,
evenings so clear, they're blue,
at your door I bury my steps
and you don't come to your door.

No window in your door
through which to speak to you.
Evening, a remote grace
that I shall never have.

And the blue evening crowns
your door so empty, it's grey.
And night grows ever bigger
with no hope of day.

43

Rumorosas pestañas
de los cañaverales.
Cayendo sobre el sueño
del hombre hasta dejarle
el pecho apaciguado
y la cabeza suave.

Ahogad la voz del arma,
que no despierte y salte
con el cuchillo de odio
que entre sus dientes late.

Así, dormido, el hombre
toda la tierra vale.

44

Fue una alegría de una sola vez,
de esas que no son nunca más iguales.
El corazón, lleno de historias tristes,
fue arrebatado por las claridades.

Fue una alegría como la mañana,
que puso azul el corazón, y grande,
más comunicativo su latido,
más esbelta su cumbre aleteante.

Fue una alegría que dolió de tanto
encenderse, reírse, dilatarse.
Una mujer y yo la recogimos
desde un niño rodado de su carne.

Fue una alegría en el amanecer
más virginal de todas las verdades.
Se inflamaban los gallos, y callaron
atravesados por su misma sangre.

43

Rushing eyelashes
of the reed fields.
Heavy on man's sleep
until his breast
remains appeased
and his head calm.

Stifle the weapon's voice,
so he does not wake up and leap
with the knife of hatred
throbbing between his teeth.

Thus, asleep, man is worth
all the earth.

44

It was a joy for once only,
never to be repeated.
The heart, full of sad stories,
was seized by clarity.

It was a joy as of morning;
it azured, expanded the heart,
made its beat more resounding,
trimmer its fluttering peak.

It was a joy that pained for its
sheer flashing, laughing, expanding.
A woman and I gathered it
from the child of her flesh moulded.

It was a joy in the most virginal
dawning of all truths.
The cocks caught fire and fell silent
transfixed by their own blood.

Fue la primera vez de la alegría
la sola vez de su total imagen.
Las otras alegrías se quedaron
como granos de arena ante los mares.

Fue una alegría para siempre sola,
para siempre dorada, destellante.
Pero es una tristeza para siempre,
porque apenas nacida fue a enterrarse.

45

VIDA SOLAR

Cuerpo de claridad que nada empaña.
Todo es materia de cristal radiante,
a través de ese sol que te acompaña,
que te lleva por dentro hacia adelante.

Carne de limpidez enardecida,
hueso más transparente si más hondo,
piel hacia el sur del fuego dirigida.
Sangre resplandeciente desde el fondo.

Cuerpo diurno, día sobrehumano,
fruto del cegador acoplamiento,
de una áurea madrugada del verano
con el más inflamado firmamento.

Ígnea ascensión, sangrienta hacia los montes,
agua sólida y ágil hacia el día,
diáfano barro lleno de horizontes,
coronación astral de la alegría.

It was joy's first time,
a once only of its total image.
Other joys lay
as sand-grains by the seas.

It was a joy ever once only,
ever golden, glistening.
But it is sadness for ever;
just born, it was buried.

45

SOLAR LIFE

Body of a clarity nothing can mist.
Everything is of radiant crystal,
through that sun that accompanies you,
that bears you inside forward.

Flesh of inflamed cleanness,
bone more transparent though deeper,
skin pointed towards the south of fire.
Blood shining from the depth.

Daytime body, superhuman day,
fruit of the blind coupling,
of a golden summer morning
with the most inflamed sky.

A flaming ascent, bloody towards the mountains,
water solid and agile towards the day,
diaphanous clay full of horizons,
astral crowning of happiness.

Cuerpo como un solsticio de arcos plenos,
bóveda plena, plenas llamaradas.
Todos los cuerpos fulgen más morenos
bajo el cenit de todas tus miradas.

Cuerpo de polen férvido y dorado,
flexible y rumoroso, tuyo y mío.
De la noche final me has enlutado,
del amor, del cabello más sombrío.

Ilumina el abismo donde lloro
por la consumación de las espumas.
Fúndete con la sombra que atesoro
hasta que en transparencias te consumas.

46

Entusiasmo del odio,
ojos del mal querer.
Turbio es el hombre,
turbia la mujer.

47

¿Qué pasa?
Rencor por tu mundo,
amor por mi casa.

¿Qué suena?
El tiro en tu monte,
y el beso en mis eras.

¿Qué viene?
Para ti una sola,
para mí dos muertes.

Body like a solstice of full arches,
a full vault, full blazes.
All bodies shine darker
under the zenith of your gazes

Body of passionate and golden pollen,
flexible and noisy, yours and mine.
You have darkened me with final night,
with love, with darker hair.

Light up the abyss where I weep
for the consummation of froth.
Fuse yourself with the shadow I hoard
until you are consumed in transparencies.

46

Hatred's ebullience.
Unlove's eyes.
Man is murky.
Woman as well.

47

What's astir?
In your world, rancour;
at my house, love.

What's that noise?
Shooting in your thicket,
kissing on my threshing floors.

What approaches?
For you, one death;
two for me.

48

Corazón de leona
tienes a veces.
Zarpa, nardo del odio,
siempre floreces.

Una leona
llevaré cada día
como corona.

49

La vejez en los pueblos.
El corazón sin dueño.
El amor sin objeto.
La hierba, el polvo, el cuervo.
¿Y la juventud?
En el ataúd.

El árbol solo y seco.
La mujer como un leño
de viudez sobre el lecho.
El odio sin remedio.
¿Y la juventud?
En el ataúd.

48

Yours is often
a lioness heart.
Paw, hatred's nard,
you'll always flower.

Day by day
I'll wear a lioness
as my crown.

49

Old age in villages.
The heart unmastered.
Love aimless.
Grass, dust, raven.
And what of youth?
In the coffin.

The tree alone and dead.
On the bed a woman
in widowed stiffness.
Ineluctable hatred.
And what of youth?
In the coffin.

50

Llueve. Los ojos se ahondan
buscando tus ojos: esos
dos ojos que se alejaron
a la sombra cuenca adentro.
Mirada con horizontes
cálidos y fondos tiernos,
íntimamente alentada
por un sol de íntimo fuego
que era en las pestañas, negra
coronación de los sueños.

Mirada negra y dorada,
hecha de dardos directos,
signo de un alma en lo alto
de todo lo verdadero.

Ojos que se han consumado
infinitamente abiertos
hacia el saber que vivir
es llevar la luz a un centro.

Llueve como si llorara
raudales un ojo inmenso,
un ojo gris, desangrado,
pisoteado en el cielo.

Llueve sobre tus dos ojos
que pisan hasta los perros.
Llueve sobre tus dos ojos
negros, negros, negros, negros,
y llueve como si el agua
verdes quisiera volverlos.

Pero sus arcos prosiguen
alejándose y hundiendo
negrura frutal en todo
el corazón de lo negro.

50

It's raining. Eyes sink
in search of your eyes, those
two eyes that sank away
into the shadow, down their sockets.
A gaze with warm
horizons and gentle depths,
fanned within
by a sun of inner fire,
a crowning of dreams
in the black eyelashes.

A black and gilded gaze,
all sure-struck arrows,
sign of a soul surmounting
what truths there are.

Eyes that have been fulfilled
infinitely open
to the knowledge that to live
is to bear the light to a centre.

It's raining as if an immense
eye wept torrents,
a grey eye, bled-white,
trampled in the sky.

It's raining over your two eyes
which even the dogs trample.
It's raining over your two eyes,
black, black, black, black,
and it's raining as if the water
would turn them green.

But their arches go on
moving away and sinking
a fruitlike blackness
in all the heart of darkness.

¿Volverán a florecer?
Si a través de tantos cuerpos
que ya combaten la flor
renovaran su ascua... Pero
seguirán bajo la lluvia
para siempre mustios, secos

51

Era un hoyo no muy hondo.
Casi en la flor de la sombra.
No hubiera cabido un hombre
en su oscuridad angosta.
Contigo todo fue anchura
en la tierra tenebrosa.

Mi casa contigo era
la habitación de la bóveda.
Dentro de mi casa entraba
por ti la luz victoriosa.

Mi casa va siendo un hoyo.
Yo no quisiera que toda
aquella luz se alejara
vencida, desde la alcoba.

Pero cuando llueve, siento
que las paredes se ahondan,
y reverdecen los muebles,
rememorando las hojas.

Mi casa es una ciudad
con una puerta a la aurora,
otra más grande a la tarde,
y a la noche, inmensa, otra.

Mi casa es un ataúd.
Bajo la lluvia redobla.
Y ahuyenta las golondrinas
que no la quisieran torva.

Will they flower again?
If across as many dead
as combat flowers,
they would glow afresh ... But
they will stay under the rain
forever withered, shrivelled.

51

It was a hollow not too deep.
Almost the depth of a shadow.
A man would scarcely fit
into its narrow darkness.
With you all became width
on the darkened earth.

With you my house was
a dwelling in the dome.
Triumphant light, through you,
flooded into my house.

My house is turning to a pit.
I would not have
all that light abandon
the alcove, in defeat.

But when it rains, I feel
that the walls strike root,
and the furniture burgeons again,
remembering its leaves.

My house is a town
with one gate to dawn,
another, greater, to evening,
and to night another, immense.

My house is a coffin.
It drums under the rain
and chases the swallows
that dislike its frown.

En mi casa falta un cuerpo.
Dos en nuestra casa sobran.

52

A MI HIJO

Te has negado a cerrar los ojos, muerto mío,
abiertos ante el cielo como dos golondrinas:
su color coronado de junios, ya es rocío
alejándose a ciertas regiones matutinas.

Hoy, que es un día como bajo la tierra, oscuro,
como bajo la tierra, lluvioso, despoblado,
con la humedad sin sol de mi cuerpo futuro,
como bajo la tierra quiero haberte enterrado.

Desde que tú eres muerto no alientan las mañanas,
al fuego arrebatadas de tus ojos solares:
precipitado octubre contra nuestras ventanas,
diste paso al otoño y anocheció los mares.

Te ha devorado el sol, rival único y hondo
y la remota sombra que te lanzó encendido;
te empuja luz abajo llevándote hasta el fondo,
tragándote; ya es como si no hubieras nacido.

Diez meses en la luz, redondeando el cielo,
sol muerto, anochecido, sepultado, eclipsado.
Sin pasar por el día se marchitó tu pelo;
atardeció tu carne con el alba en un lado.

El pájaro pregunta por ti, cuerpo al oriente,
carne naciente al alba y al júbilo precisa;
niño que sólo supo reír, tan largamente,
que sólo ciertas flores mueren con tu sonrisa.

In my house one body is missing.
Two in our house: too many.

52

TO MY SON

You have refused to close your eyes, my dead one,
open before the sky like two swallows:
their colour crowned with Junes, is now dew
fading away into certain morning regions.

Today, which is a day as under the earth, dark,
as under the earth, rainy, deserted,
with the sunless humidity of my future body,
as under the earth I wish to have you buried.

Since you are dead, the mornings don't breathe,
snatched from the fire of your solar eyes:
October hurled against our windows,
you gave way to autumn and it darkened the seas.

The sun has devoured you, only and profound rival
and the remote shadow, a fireball, hurled you;
light pushed you down carrying you to the depths,
swallowing you up; and it is as if you were not born.

Ten months of life, rounding the sky,
dead sun, nighted, buried, eclipsed.
Without passing the day, your hair withered;
your flesh eveninged with the dawn on one side.

The bird asks for you, body to the east,
flesh that's born at dawn and that's it;
child who only knew how to laugh, so lengthily,
that only certain flowers die with your smile.

Ausente, ausente, ausente como la golondrina,
ave estival que esquiva vivir al pie del hielo:
golondrina que a poco de abrir la pluma fina,
naufraga en las tijeras enemigas del vuelo.

Flor que no fue capaz de endurecer los dientes,
de llegar al más leve signo de la fiereza.
Vida como una hoja de labios incipientes,
hoja que se desliza cuando a sonar empieza.

Los consejos del mar de nada te han valido...
Vengo de dar a un tierno sol una puñalada,
de enterrar un pedazo de pan en el olvido,
de echar sobre unos ojos un puñado de nada.

Verde, rojo, moreno: verde, azul y dorado;
los latentes colores de la vida, los huertos,
el centro de las flores a tus pies destinado,
de oscuros negros tristes, de graves blancos yertos.

Mujer arrinconada: mira que ya es de día.
(¡Ay, ojos sin poniente por siempre en la alborada!)
Pero en tu vientre, pero en tus ojos, mujer mía,
la noche continúa cayendo desolada.

Absent, absent, absent like the swallow,
summer bird who shuns living at the foot of ice:
swallow who soon after opening its fine plumage,
is shipwrecked in the hostile shears of its flight.

Flower unable to toughen its teeth,
of arriving at the lighter side of wildness.
Life like a leaf of incipient lips,
leaf that glides when it begins to sound.

The sea's advice has been worthless to you ...
I come from stabbing a tender sun,
from burying a piece of bread in oblivion,
from throwing over some eyes a handful of nothing.

Green, red, brown: green, blue and gold;
the latent colours of life, the orchard-gardens,
the centre of flowers meant for your feet,
dark black sad; grave, white, inert.

Isolated woman: see, it is now daylight.
(Ah, unsetting eyes always at dawn!)
But in your womb, but in your eyes, woman of mine,
night continues falling desolate.

53

ORILLAS DE TU VIENTRE

¿Qué exaltaré en la tierra que no sea algo tuyo?
A mi lecho de ausente me echo como a una cruz
de solitarias lunas del deseo, y exalto
la orilla de tu vientre.

Clavellina del valle que provocan tus piernas.
Granada que has rasgado de plenitud su boca.
Trémula zarzamora suavemente dentada
donde vivo arrojado.

Arrojado y fugaz como el pez generoso,
ansioso de que el agua, la lenta acción del agua
lo devaste: sepulte su decisión eléctrica
de fértiles relámpagos.

Aún me estremece el choque primero de los dos;
cuando hicimos pedazos la luna a dentelladas,
impulsamos la sábanas a un abril de amapolas,
nos inspiraba el mar.

Soto que atrae, umbría de vello casi en llamas,
dentellada tenaz que siento en lo más hondo,
vertiginoso abismo que me recoge, loco
de la lúcida muerte.

Túnel por el que a ciegas me aferro a tus entrañas.
Recóndito lucero tras una madreselva
hacia donde la espuma se agolpa, arrebatada
del íntimo destino.

En ti tiene el oasis su más ansiado huerto:
el clavel y el jazmín se entrelazan, se ahogan.
De ti son tantos siglos de muerte, de locura
como te han sucedido.

53

THE SHORES OF YOUR WOMB

What shall I exalt on the earth that is not yours?
I throw myself on my bed of absence as on a cross
of solitary moons of desire, and I exalt
the shore of your womb.

Pinks of the valley that your legs provoke.
Pomegranate whose fullness tore open its mouth.
Quivering blackberry gently teethed
where, thrown, I live.

Hurled and fleet as the lavish fish,
eager to be worn down by the water,
the slow action of water
eager to bury, sink its electric will of fertile lightnings.

Our first clash still shakes me;
the sea inspired us
when we chewed up the moon,
when we pressed the bedsheets to an April of poppies.

An alluring thicket, shade of hair almost in flames,
a stubborn bite I feel in my depths,
vertiginous abyss that catches me, wild
with lucid death.

Tunnel through which blindfolded I clasp your innards.
Hidden bright star filtered through honeysuckle
towards which the foam leaps, snatched
from its intimate fate.

In you the oasis has its most desired orchard:
carnation and jasmine entwine, choke.
Centuries of death are yours, of madness
which have befallen you.

Corazón de la tierra, centro del universo,
todo se atorbellina, con afán de satélite
en torno a ti, pupila del sol que te entreabres
en la flor del manzano.

Ventana que da al mar, a una diáfana muerte
cada vez más profunda, más azul y anchurosa.
Su hálito de infinito propaga los espacios
entre tú y yo y el fuego.

Trágame, leve hoyo donde avanzo y me entierro.
La losa que me cubra sea tu vientre leve,
la madera tu carne, la bóveda tu ombligo,
la eternidad la orilla.

En ti me precipito como en la inmensidad
de un mediodía claro de sangre submarina.
mientras el delirante hoyo se hunde en el mar,
y el clamor se hace hombre.

Por ti logro en tu centro la libertad del astro.
En ti nos acoplamos como dos eslabones,
tú poseedora y yo. Y así somos cadena:
mortalmente abrazados.

54

Todo está lleno de ti,
y todo de mí está lleno:
llenas están las ciudades,
igual que los cementerios
de ti, por todas las casas,
de mí, por todos los cuerpos.

Por las calles voy dejando
algo que voy recogiendo:
pedazos de vida mía
venidos desde muy lejos.

Heart of the earth, centre of the universe,
everything a whirlwind, a satellite
around you, the sun's eye opening
in the bloom of the apple tree.

Window to the sea, to a translucent death
ever deeper, ever bluer and vaster.
Its infinite breath spreads the spaces
among you and me and fire.

Swallow me, light hollow where I advance and am buried.
Let your light belly be a slab to cover me,
your flesh timber, your navel the vault,
the shore eternity.

I hurl myself down into you as into an immensity
of a bright noon of submarine blood,
while the delirious hollow sinks in the sea,
and the clamour becomes man.

Through you, in your centre, I achieve the star's freedom,
like two chainlinks we fit together, possessor
and possessed. And so we are a chain:
mortally embraced.

54

Everything is full of you,
and everything is full of me:
the towns are full
as well as the graveyards
of you - all the houses,
of me all - the bodies.

Along the streets I leave
something I pick up as I go:
bits of my life
that have come from afar.

Voy alado a la agonía,
arrastrándome me veo
en el umbral, en el fondo
latente del nacimiento.

Todo está lleno de mí:
de algo que es tuyo y recuerdo
perdido, pero encontrado
alguna vez, algún tiempo.

Tiempo que se queda atrás
decididamente negro,
indeleblemente rojo,
dorado sobre tu cuerpo.

Todo está lleno de ti,
traspasado de tu pelo:
de algo que no he conseguido
y que busco entre tus huesos.

55

Callo después de muerto.
Hablas después de viva.
Pobres conversaciones
desusadas por dichas,
nos llevan lo mejor
de la muerte y la vida.

Con espadas fraguadas
en silencio, fundidas
en miradas, en besos,
en pasiones, invictas
nos herimos, nos vamos
a la lucha más íntima.
Con silencio te ataco.
Con silencio tú vibras.
Con silencio reluce
la verdad cristalina.

I wing my way to an agony,
I'm aware of dragging myself
on the threshold, on the latent
bottom of the wellspring.

Everything is full of me:
of something yours and
a memory lost, but found
once, some time.

Time that's left behind,
decidedly black,
indelibly red,
gilded over your body.

Everything is full of you,
pierced by your hair:
of something I haven't found
and I seek among your bones.

55

A dead man, I stay silent.
A living woman, you speak.
Poor conversations,
too long heard to be of use,
bear off the best
of death and of life.

With tempered swords beaten
in silence, smelted
in looks, in kisses,
in untamed passions,
we are wounded, we are off
to the innermost combat.
With quiet I attack you.
With quiet you throb.
With quiet crystalline
truth sparkles.

Con silencio caemos
en la noche, en el día.

56

La libertad es algo
que sólo en tus entrañas
bate como el relámpago.

57

Cuerpo sobre cuerpo,
tierra sobre tierra:
viento sobre viento.

58

Bocas de ira.
Ojos de acecho.
Perros aullando.
Perros y perros.
Todo baldío.
Todo reseco.
Cuerpos y campos,
cuerpos y cuerpos.

¡Qué mal camino,
qué ceniciento
corazón tuyo,
fértil y tierno!

Quietly we fall
over day, over night.

56

Freedom is something
that only in your innards
strikes like lightning.

57

Body upon body,
earth upon earth,
wind upon wind.

58

Angry mouths.
Stalking eyes.
Howling dogs.
Dogs and dogs.
All barren.
All parched.
Bodies and fields,
bodies and bodies.

What a bad road!
How ashen
heart of yours,
fertile and soft!

59

Tristes guerras
si no es amor la empresa.
Tristes. Tristes.

Tristes armas
si no son las palabras.
Tristes. Tristes.

Tristes hombres
si no mueren de amores.
Tristes. Tristes.

60

Los animales del día
a los de la noche buscan.

Lejos anda el sol,
cerca la luna.

Animal del mediodía,
la medianoche te turba.

Lejos anda el sol.
Cerca la luna.

59

Doleful wars
if love is not the enterprise.
Doleful, doleful.

Doleful weapons
if they are not words.
Doleful, doleful.

Doleful men
if they die not for love.
Doleful, doleful.

60

The animals of day
seek those of night.

The sun is away,
the night close by.

Mid-day animal,
midnight disturbs you.

The sun is away,
the moon close by.

61

HIJO DE LA LUZ Y DE LA SOMBRA

I

(HIJO DE LA SOMBRA)

Eres la noche, esposa: la noche en el instante
mayor de su potencia lunar y femenina.
Eres la medianoche: la sombra culminante
donde culmina el sueño, donde el amor culmina.

Forjado por el día, mi corazón que quema
lleva su gran pisada de sol adonde quieres,
con un solar impulso, con una luz suprema,
cumbre de las mañanas y los atardeceres.

Daré sobre tu cuerpo cuando la noche arroje
su avaricioso anhelo de imán y poderío.
Un astral sentimiento febril me sobrecoge,
incendia mi osamenta con un escalofrío.

El aire de la noche desordena tus pechos,
y desordena y vuelca los cuerpos con su choque.
Como una tempestad de enloquecidos lechos,
eclipsa la parejas, las hace un solo bloque.

La noche se ha encendido como una sorda hoguera
de llamas minerales y oscuras embestidas.
Y alrededor la sombra late como si fuera
las almas de los pozos y el vino difundidas.

Ya la sombra es el nido cerrado, incandescente,
la visible ceguera puesta sobre quien ama;
ya provoca el abrazo cerrado, ciegamente,
ya recoge en sus cuevas cuanto la luz derrama.

La sombra pide, exige seres que se entrelacen,
besos que la constelen de relámpagos largos,
bocas embravecidas, batidas, que atenacen,
arrullos que hagan música de sus mudos letargos.

61

SON OF THE LIGHT AND DARKNESS

I

(SON OF DARKNESS)

You are the night, spouse: night at the point
of its greatest power, lunar and feminine.
You are midnight: culminant dark
where sleep culminates, where love culminates.

Wrought by the day, my heart that burns
brings its large footprint to the place you want,
with a solar urge, with a supreme light,
the summit of mornings and evenings.

I shall fall on your body when night will cast
its greedy keenness of magnet and might.
A feverish astral feeling overwhelms me,
inflames my bones with a shiver.

The night air unsettles your breasts,
it knocks, unsettles and overturns bodies.
Like a storm of maddened beds
it eclipses couples, makes them a single lump.

The night is alight as a dimmed bonfire
of mineral flames and dark charges.
And round about the shadows beat as
wells whose souls have spilled and wine.

Darkness is now the fastened nest, red-hot,
the visible blindness laid on one who loves;
it may prompt a tight embrace, blindly,
it may hoard in its caves all that light spouts.

Shadow requires, exacts beings that entwine,
kisses that constellate it with lengthy flashes,
wild, spurred-on mouths that lock,
lullabies that turn to music their mute lethargies.

Pide que nos echemos tú y yo sobre la manta,
tú y yo sobre la luna, tú y yo sobre la vida.
Pide que tú y yo ardamos fundiendo en la garganta,
con todo el firmamento, la tierra estremecida.

El hijo está en la sombra que acumula luceros,
amor, tuétano, luna, claras oscuridades.
Brota de sus perezas y de sus agujeros,
y de sus solitarias y apagadas ciudades.

El hijo está en la sombra: de la sombra ha surtido,
y a su origen infunden los astros una siembra,
un zumo lácteo, un flujo de cálido latido,
que ha de obligar sus huesos al sueño y a la hembra.

Moviendo está la sombra sus fuerzas siderales,
tendiendo está la sombra su constelada umbría,
volcando las parejas y haciéndolas nupciales.
Tú eres la noche, esposa. Yo soy el mediodía.

II

(HIJO DE LA LUZ)

Tú eres el alba, esposa: la principal penumbra,
recibes entornadas las horas de tu frente.
Decidido al fulgor, pero entornado, alumbra
tu cuerpo. Tus entrañas forjan el sol naciente.

Centro de claridades, la gran hora te espera
en el umbral de un fuego que el fuego mismo abrasa:
te espero yo, inclinado como el trigo a la era,
colocando en el centro de la luz nuestra casa.

La noche desprendida de los pozos oscuros,
se sumerge en los pozos donde ha echado raíces.
Y tú te abres al parto luminoso, entre muros
que se rasgan contigo como pétreas matrices.

It demands that the two of us lie on the blanket,
you and I on the moonshine, you and I upon life.
It bids you and me flare up, whilst in our throats
we blend the quivering earth with the whole firmament.

The son is in the shadows that hoard morning stars,
love, marrow, moonshine, all illumined darkness.
He sprouts from the dark's sloth, from the dark's pores,
from its lonesome and dulled cities.

The son is in the shadows: he has sprung out of the dark,
and his beginning is seeded by the stars,
a milky sap, a fluid of warm beat
that shall compel his bones to sleep and the female.

The dark is wielding its sidereal powers,
the shadows are casting their constellated shade,
upturning couples and making them nuptial.
You are night, spouse. I am midday.

II

(SON OF LIGHT)

You are dawn, spouse: a foremost twilight,
at a slant you catch the hours of your forehead.
Resolved to radiance, but slanting, your body
shines. Your innards mould the rising sun.

On the threshold of a fire-consuming fire
the great hour awaits you, core of all that shines:
I await you, prone as wheat towards the threshing-floor,
while I place our house in the light's core.

Night, cut loose of its dark wells,
sinks down wells in which it has struck root.
And you are exposed to a luminous birthing, between walls
that are rended with you like wombs of rock.

La gran hora del parto, la más rotunda hora:
estallan los relojes sintiendo tu alarido,
se abren todas las puertuas del mundo, de la aurora,
y el sol nace en tu vientre donde encontró su nido.

El hijo fue primero sombra y ropa cosida
por tu corazón hondo desde tus hondas manos.
Con sombras y con ropas anticipó su vida,
con sombras y con ropas de gérmenes humanos.

Las sombras y las ropas sin población, desiertas,
se han poblado de un niño sonoro, un movimiento,
que en nuestra casa pone de par en par las puertas,
y ocupa en ella a gritos el luminoso asiento.

¡Ay, la vida: qué hermoso penar tan moribundo!
Sombras y ropas trajo la del hijo que nombras.
Sombras y ropas llevan los hombres por el mundo.
Y todos dejan siempre sombras: ropas y sombras.

Hijo del alba eres, hijo del mediodía.
Y han de quedar de ti luces en todo impuestas,
mientras tu madre y yo vamos a la agonía,
dormidos y despiertos con el amor a cuestas.

Hablo y el corazón me sale en el aliento.
Si no hablara lo mucho que quiero me ahogaría.
Con espliego y resinas perfumo tu aposento.
Tú eres el alba, esposa. Yo soy el mediodía.

III

(HIJO DE LA LUZ Y DE LA SOMBRA)

Tejidos en el alma, grabados, dos panales
no pueden detener la miel en los pezones.
Tus pechos en el alba: maternos manantiales,
luchan y se atropellan con blancas efusiones.

The great hour of childbirth, the squarest hour:
clocks burst on hearing your shriek,
the world's, dawn's gates are all flung open,
and over your womb, where it had found its nest, the sun rises.

The boy was first shadow and clothing sewn
by your profound heart out of your profound hands.
With shadows and with clothes he lived ahead of himself,
the shadow and the clothes of human seeding.

Unpeopled, deserted shadows and clothes
were inhabited by a sounding boy, by a bustle
that opens wide all doors in our house
and, shouting, takes his shining seat in it.

Ah, life! such a glorious pain, so death-like!
your son's - the son you name - bright shadows and clothes!
People carry shadows and clothes round about the world
and they all leave always shadows: clothes and shadows.

You are dawn's son, the son of noon.
And lights imposed all over is what you shall leave behind,
while your mother and I make headway towards agony,
shouldering our love whether awake or asleep.

I speak breathing out my heart.
I would choke, should I not speak all I want.
With lavender and resin I scent your lodge.
You are dawn, spouse. I am midday.

III

(SON OF LIGHT AND DARKNESS)

Imprinted, woven into the soul, two honeycombs
cannot contain the honey of your nipples.
Your breasts in the dawn: maternal wellsprings,
they struggle and collide amid white effusions.

Se han desbordado, esposa, lunarmente tus venas,
hasta inundar la casa que tu sabor rezuma.
Y es como si brotaras de un pueblo de colmenas,
tú eres una colmena de leche con espuma.

Es como si tu sangre fuera dulzura toda,
laboriosas abejas filtradas por tus poros.
Oigo un clamor de leche, de inundación, de boda
junto a ti, recorrida por caudales sonoros.

Caudalosa mujer, en tu vientre me entierro.
Tu caudaloso vientre será mi sepultura.
Si quemaran mis huesos con la llama del hierro,
verían qué grabada llevo allí tu figura.

Para siempre fundidos en el hijo quedamos:
fundidos como anhelan nuestras ansias voraces:
en un ramo de tiempo, de sangre, los dos ramos,
en un haz de caricias, de pelo, los dos haces.

Los muertos, con un fuego congelado que abrasa,
laten junto a los vivos de una manera terca.
Viene a ocupar el hijo los campos y la casa
que tú y yo abandonamos quedándonos muy cerca.

Haremos de este hijo generador sustento,
y hará de nuestra carne materia decisiva:
donde sienten su alma las manos y el aliento
las hélices circulen, la agricultura viva.

Él hará que esta vida no caiga derribada,
pedazo desprendido de nuestros dos pedazos,
que de nuestras dos bocas hará una sola espada
y dos brazos eternos de nuestros cuatro brazos.

No te quiero a ti sola: te quiero en tu ascendencia
y en cuanto de tu vientre descenderá mañana.
Porque la especie humana me han dado por herencia
la familia del hijo será la especie humana.

Spouse, your veins brim over like moonshine
till they swamp a house that exudes your flavour.
And it's as though you sprang out of a hive-swarm,
all of you a single bee-hive of frothy milk.

It's as though all of your blood were ambrosia,
industrious bees squeezing through all your pores.
I hear a din of milk, of flood, of wedding-feast
near you, over whom loud streams course.

Overflowing woman, I'm buried in your womb.
Your overflowing womb shall be my grave.
Should they light my bones with the iron's flame,
they would see your likeness engraved there so deep.

We are both forever cast in our son:
fused, as desired by our voracious craving:
two posies in one, one of time, of blood,
one hair sheaf of caresses, the two sheaves.

The dead, in a frozen blazing fire,
throb near the living with stubborn beat.
The sun comes to enter these fields, that house
we left, even while halting all too close.

Of this son we shall make quickening sustenance,
and of our flesh he shall make accomplished matter:
where hands and breath shall feel his soul,
there propellers, living farm-work shall thrive.

He shall compel this life not to collapse,
a lump coming loose off our two lumps,
for he shall fashion one single sword with our two mouths
and two everlasting arms with our four.

It's not you alone I love: I love you in your ancestors
and in what tomorrow will come down from your womb.
Since I have been made by humankind's legacy,
my son's household will be humankind.

Con el amor a cuestas, dormidos y despiertos,
seguiremos besándonos en el hijo profundo.
Besándonos tú y yo se besan nuestros muertos
se besan los primeros pobladores del mundo.

62

(LA LLUVIA)

Ha enmudecido el campo, presintiendo la lluvia.
Reaparece en la tierra su primer abandono.
La alegría del cielo se desconsuela a veces,
sobre un pastor sediento.

Cuando la lluvia llama se remueven los muertos.
La tierra se hace un hoyo removido, oloroso.
Los árboles exhalan su último olor profundo
dispuestos a morirse.

Bajo la lluvia adquiere la voz de los relojes
la gravedad, la angustia de la postrera hora.
Reviven las heridas visibles y otras
que sangran hacia dentro.

Todo se hace entrañable, reconcentrado, íntimo.
Como bajo el subsuelo, bajo el signo lluvioso.
Todo, todo parece desear ahora
la paz definitiva.

Llueve como una sangre transparente, hechizada.
Me siento traspasado por la humedad del suelo
que habrá de sujetarme para siempre a la sombra,
para siempre a la lluvia.

El cielo se desangra pausadamente herido.
El verde intensifica la penumbra en las hojas.
Los troncos y los muertos se oscurecen aún más
por la pasión del agua.

Asleep or awake we shoulder our love,
we shall keep kissing deep within our son.
When you and I kiss, then our dead kiss too,
the earliest dwellers of the world kiss.

62

THE RAIN

The countryside's struck dumb, while rain persists.
The earth's first abandonment returns.
Heaven's joy turns desolate at times
over a thirsting shepherd.

When rain calls, the dead stir.
The earth becomes a loose, fragrant hollow.
Trees exhale their last deep odour
in readiness for dying.

Under the rain, the voice of clocks takes on
the gravity, the anguish of a last parting-hour.
Wounds visible and inward bleeding
are both revived.

Under the rain's spell all turns
endearing, pensive, intimate as if underground.
All, all seems to crave now
a definitive peace.

Rain falls as would bewitched, transparent blood.
I feel soaked through by the ground's damp
that shall forever bind me to the shadows,
forever to the rain.

Haltingly wounded heaven bleeds away.
The green enhances the twilight of the leafage.
The tree-stumps darken ever more
for the passion of water.

Y retoñan las cartas viejas en los rincones
que olvido bajo el sol. Los besos de anteayer,
las maderas más y resecas, los muertos
retoñan cuando llueve.

Bodegas, pozos, almas, saben a más hundidos.
Inundas, casi sepultados, mis sentimientos,
tú, que, brumosa, inmóvil pareces el fantasma
de tu fotografía.

Música de la lluvia, de la muerte, del sueño,
....
Todos los animales, fatídicos,
debajo de las gotas.

Suena en las hojas secas igual que en las esquinas,
suena en el mar la lluvia como en un imposible.
Suena dentro del surco como en un vientre seco,
seco, sordo, baldío.

Suena en las hondonadas y en los barrancos: suena
como una pasión íntima suicidada o ahogada.
Suena como las balas penetrando la carne,
como el llanto de todos.

Redoblan sus tambores, tañe su flauta lenta,
su lagrimosa lengua que lame tercamente.
Y siempre suena como sobre los ataúdes,
los dolores, la nada.

And letters long exchanged emit fresh shoots
in corners I forget under the sun. Kisses of before yesterday,
the dried wood ever older, the dead too
shoot up again, when rain falls.

Cellars, wells, souls taste as if sunk deeper.
Hazy, motionless, you that look like your own
photo's ghost, flood my
all but buried feelings.

Rain's, death's, sleep's music ,
....
Fatestruck, all animals are bowed down
under the raindrops.

It sounds on dead eaves as on street corners,
rain sounds on the sea as it would on the impossible.
Inside the furrow it sounds as in a womb,
a dried, dull, barren one.

It sounds in the gorges and ravines; it sounds
as an intimate self-slaughtered or smothered passion.
It sounds like bullets piercing flesh,
like the weeping of all.

Its drums beat, its slow flute, its tearful,
stubbornly lapping tongue moans.
And it ever sounds as if on caskets,
sorrows, nothingness.

63

Menos tu vientre,
todo es confuso.
Menos tu vientre,
todo es futuro,
fugaz, pasado
baldío, turbio.
Menos tu vientre,
todo es oculto.
Menos tu vientre,
todo inseguro,
todo postrero,
polvo sin mundo.
Menos tu vientre
todo es oscuro.
Menos tu vientre
claro y profundo.

64

ANTES DEL ODIO

Beso soy, sombra con sombra.
Beso, dolor con dolor,
por haberme enamorado,
corazón sin corazón,
de las cosas, del aliento
sin sombra de la creación.
Sed con agua en la distancia,
pero sed alrededor.

Corazón en una copa
donde me lo bebo yo,
y no se lo bebe nadie,
nadie sabe su sabor.
Odio, vida: ¡cuánto odio
sólo por amor!

63

Save for your womb
all is dim.
Save for your womb
all is future,
fleeting, past
barren, foul.
Save for your womb
all is secret.
Save for your womb
all is unsafe,
all is bygone,
unearthly dust.
Save for your womb
all is dark;
save for your clear
and deep womb.

64

BEFORE HATING

I am all kiss, shade to shade.
Kiss, pain to pain,
for, heartless heart,
I fell in love
with things, creation's
untainted breath.
Thirst, in sight of water,
yet thirst, all around.

Outpoured heart
that I, not any other,
drink;
no one knows its taste.
Hatred, love: such hatred
for love alone.

No es posible acariciarte
con las manos que me dio
el fuego de más deseo,
el ansia de más ardor.
Varias alas, varios vuelos
abaten en ellas hoy
hierros que cercan las venas
y las muerden con rencor.
Por amor, vida, abatido,
pájaro sin remisión.
Sólo por amor odiado.
Sólo por amor.

Amor, tu bóveda arriba
y yo abajo siempre, amor,
sin otra luz que estas ansias,
sin otra iluminación.
Mírame aquí encadenado,
escupido, sin calor,
a los pies de la tiniebla
más súbita, más feroz,
comiendo pan y cuchillo
como buen trabajador
y a veces cuchillo sólo,
sólo por amor.

Todo lo que significa
golondrinas, ascensión,
claridad, anchura, aire,
decidido espacio, sol,
horizonte aleteante,
sepultado en un rincón.
Esperanza, mar, desierto,
sangre, monte rodador:
libertades de mi alma
clamorosas de pasión,
desfilando por mi cuerpo,
donde no se quedan, no,
pero donde se despliegan,

No way to caress you
with hands given by the fire
of ever greater passion,
by an ever growing ardour.
Irons that seize the veins and
bite on them with rancour,
hinder now
various wings, various flights.
A felled bird, love,
felled by love, helplessly.
Hated only for love,
for love alone.

Love, your dome above
and I always below, love
with no light but this longing,
with no other light.
Here I stand bound,
spat on, robbed of warmth
at the feet of most sudden,
fiercest darkness,
eating, like any jack,
his bread and knife,
and sometimes only knife,
for love alone.

Whatever signifies
swallows, ascent,
clarity, breadth, air,
frank space, sun,
quivering horizon,
all buried in a corner.
Forest, sea, desert,
blood, rolling hill:
my soul's free rain
loud with passion
coursing through my body,
where nothing's stowed,
but all's displayed,

sólo por amor.

Porque dentro de la triste
guirnalda del eslabón,
del sabor a carcelero
constante, y a paredón,
y a precipicio en acecho,
alto, alegre, libre soy.
Alto, alegre, libre, libre,
sólo por amor.

No, no hay cárcel para el hombre.
No podrán atarme, no.
Este mundo de cadenas
me es pequeño y exterior.
¿Quién encierra una sonrisa?
¿Quién amuralla una voz?
A los lejos tú, más sola
que la muerte, la una y yo.
A los lejos tú, sintiendo
en tus brazos mi prisión:
en tus brazos donde late
la libertad de los dos.
Libre soy, siénteme libre.
Sólo por amor.

65

Palomar del arrullo
fue la habitación.

Provocabas palomas
con el corazón.

Palomar, palomar
derribado, desierto,
sin arrullo por nunca jamás.

for love alone.

Because within my bond's
sad garland
and the constant tang
of gaoler, wall,
ensnaring chasm,
I am tall, buoyant, free.
Tall, buoyant, free, free,
for love alone.

No, there's no prison for man.
They shall not bind me, no.
This world of chains
for me is nought, extraneous.
Who will confine a smile?
Who will wall in a voice?
Far off, you, lonelier
than death, to be all alone and I.
Far off, you, feeling
my prison in your arms,
in your arms where
our freedom beats.
I am free, see, free.
For love alone.

65

The room was
a cooing dovecote.

You called up doves
with your heart.

Dovecote, dovecote,
in ruins, forsaken,
all your cooing now ended.

66

LA BOCA

Boca que arrastra mi boca:
boca que me has arrastrado:
boca que vienes de lejos
a iluminarme de rayos.
Alba que das a mis noches
un esplendor rojo y blanco.
Boca poblada de bocas:
pájaro lleno de pájaros.

Canción que vuelve las alas
hacia arriba y hacia abajo.
Muerte reducida a besos,
a sed de morir despacio,
dando a la grana sangrante
dos tremendos aletazos.
El labio de arriba el cielo
y la tierra el otro labio.

Beso que rueda en la sombra:
beso que viene rodando
desde el primer cementerio
hasta los últimos astros.
Astro que tiene tu boca
enmudecido y cerrado,
hasta que un roce celeste
hace que vibren sus párpados.

Beso que va a un porvenir
de muchachas y muchachos,
que no dejarán desiertos
ni las calles ni los campos.

¡Cuántas bocas enterradas,
sin boca, desenterramos!

66
THE MOUTH

A mouth that draws my mouth.
Mouth, you have drawn me:
you came, mouth, from far off
to make me radiant bright.
Dawn, you lend my nights
a red and white glow.
A mouthful of mouths:
a chatterbox bird.

A song that turns its wings
skyward and earthward.
Death compressed in kisses,
in a thirst of slow dying,
to the bleeding scarlet you gave
two flashing wingbeats.
The upper lip, heaven,
earth the other lip.

A kiss rolling in the shadow:
a kiss that out of the first
graveyard rolls on, ever
in pursuit of the last stars.
A star your mouth keeps
silenced and closed
until it's grazed by heaven
as an eye that blinked.

A kiss that goes to a future
of boys and girls
who shall not leave deserted
streets or fields.

How many mouths, now buried,
mouthless we disinter.

Bebo en tu boca por ellos,
brindo en tu boca por tantos
que cayeron sobre el vino
de los amorosos vasos.
Hoy son recuerdos, recuerdos,
besos distantes y amargos.

Hundo en tu boca mi vida,
oigo rumores de espacios,
y el infinito parece
que sobre mí se ha volcado.

He de volverte a besar,
he de volver, hundo, caigo,
mientras descienden los siglos
hacia los hondos barrancos
como una febril nevada
de besos y enamorados.

Boca que desenterraste
el amanecer más claro
con tu lengua. Tres palabras,
tres fuegos has heredado:
vida, muerte, amor. Ahí quedan
escritos sobre tus labios.

67

La basura diaria
que de los hombres queda
sobre mis sentimientos
y mis sentidos pesa.

Es la triste basura
de los turbios deseos,
de las pasiones turbias.

To them I drink from your mouth;
in your mouth I toast so many
who fell upon the wine
of love's goblets.
Today they are memories, memories,
kisses distant and bitter.

I sink my life in your mouth,
I hear space resound,
and it's as if the infinite
had overwhelmed me.

I shall kiss you again.
Kiss you. I plunge, I fall,
while the centuries descend
over the deep ravines
as a feverish snowfall
of kisses and lovers.

Mouth that disinterred
the clearest dawn
with your tongue. Three words,
three fires you were bequeathed:
life, death, love. There they are,
written on your lips.

67

The daily waste
of men clings
to my feelings,
weighs on my senses.

It is the sad waste
of dark longings,
of dark passions.

68

Cerca del agua te quiero llevar,
porque tu arrullo trascienda del mar.

Cerca del agua te quiero tener,
porque te aliente su vívido ser.

Cerca del agua te quiero sentir,
porque la espuma te enseñe a reír.

Cerca del agua te quiero, mujer,
ver, abarcar, fecundar, conocer.

Cerca del agua perdida del mar,
que no se puede perder ni encontrar.

69

El azahar de Murcia
y la palmera de Elche
para exaltar la vida
sobre tu vida ascienden.

El azahar de Murcia
y la palmera de Elche
para seguir la vida
bajan sobre tu muerte.

68

I will bring you near the water
so your lullaby comes from the sea.

I will have you near the water
so its briskness quickens you.

I will feel you near the water
so its froth teaches you to laugh.

I will feel you near the water, woman,
to see, encompass, seed and know you.

By the sea's forsaken water
which no one can lose or find.

69

For life's ascendance
Murcia's orange blossom
and Elche's palmtree
hang over your life.

For life's pursuance
Murcia's orange blossom
and Elche's palmtree
hang over your death.

70

ASCENSIÓN DE LA ESCOBA

Coronad a la escoba de laurel, mirto, rosa.
Es el héroe entre aquellos que afrontan la basura.
Para librar el polvo sin vuelo cada cosa
bajó, porque era palma y azul, desde la altura.

Su ardor de espada joven y alegre no reposa.
Delgada de ansiedad, pureza, sol, bravura,
azucena que barre sobre la misma fosa,
es cada vez más alta, más cálida, más pura.

Nunca: la escoba nunca será crucificada,
porque la juventud propaga su esqueleto
que es una sola flauta muda, pero sonora.

Es una sola lengua sublime y acordada.
Y ante su aliento raudo se ausenta el polvo quieto.
Y asciende una palmera, columna hacia la aurora.

71

DESPUÉS DEL AMOR

No pudimos ser. La tierra
no pudo tanto. No somos
cuanto se propuso el sol
en un anhelo remoto.
Un pie se acerca a lo claro.
En lo oscuro insiste el otro.
Porque el amor no es perpetuo
en nadie, ni en mí tampoco.
El odio aguarda su instante
dentro del carbón más hondo.
Rojo es el odio y nutrido.
El amor, pálido y solo.
Cansado de odiar, te amo.

70

ASCENT OF THE BROOM

Crown the broom of laurel, myrtle, rose.
It's the hero among those that confront rubbish.
To free the flightless dust each thing,
because it was a palm and blue, descended from the height.

Its sword-passion, young and gay, has no rest.
Thin with anxiety, purity, sun, bravery,
a lily that sweeps on its own grave,
ever taller, hotter, purer.

Never: the broom will never be crucified
because youth propagates its skeleton
which is a single flute, dumb but sonorous.

It's a single tongue sublime and cordant.
And before its rushing breath the quiet dust goes missing.
And a palmtree rises, a pillar towards daybreak.

71

AFTER LOVE

We fell short of ourselves. Earth
was unequal to the task. We are not
what in a far-off yearning
the sun purposed.
One foot nears the luminous.
The other is bent on the dark.
For in no one, nor in me,
is love forever.
Hate bides its time within
where coal lies deepest.
Hate is red and hale.
Love is pale and lone.
Tired of hating, I love you.

Cansado de amar, te odio.

Llueve tiempo, llueve tiempo.
Y un día triste entre todos,
triste por toda la tierra,
triste desde mí hasta el lobo,
dormimos y despertamos
con un tigre entre los ojos.

Piedras, hombres como piedras,
duros y plenos de encono,
chocan en el aire, donde
chocan las piedras de pronto.

Soledades que hoy rechazan
y ayer juntaban sus rostros.
Soledades que en el beso
guardan el rugido sordo.
Soledades para siempre.
Soledades sin apoyo.

Cuerpos como un mar voraz,
entrechocado, furioso.
Solitariamente atados
por el amor, por el odio,
por las venas surgen hombres,
cruzan la ciudades, torvos.

En el corazón arraiga
solitariamente todo.
Huellas sin compaña quedan
como en el agua, en el fondo.

Sólo una voz, a lo lejos,
siempre a lo lejos la oigo,
acompaña y hace ir
igual que el cuello a los hombros.

Sólo una voz me arrebata
este armazón espinoso

Tired of loving, I hate you.

Time rains down, rains down.
And one day, saddest of all,
all the earth-saddening days,
days that wolf-sadden me,
we go to sleep and wake
to a tiger between our eyes.

Stones, men like stones,
hard and full of rancour,
clash in the air where
suddenly stones clash.

Solitudes that repel today
and joined cheeks yesterday.
Solitudes that nurse
a harsh growl in the kiss.
Ever enduring solitudes.
Solitudes adrift.

Bodies like a greedy sea
clashing in fury.
In solitude bound
by love, by hatred.
Men rise out of all veins;
spiteful they cross cities.

Solitude nurtures
whatever enters the heart.
Their ground, as water,
yields to impressions.

Only, in the distance, a voice
I hear ever distant.
It attends and compels
as the neck the shoulder.

Just one voice strips me
of this prickly hide

de vello retrocedido
y erizado que me pongo.

Los secos vientos no pueden
secar los mares jugosos.
Y el corazón permanece
fresco en su cárcel de agosto
porque esa voz es el arma
más tierna de los arroyos:

«Miguel: me acuerdo de ti
después del sol y del polvo,
antes de la misma luna,
tumba de un sueño amoroso.»

Amor: aleja mi ser
de sus primeros escombros,
y edificándome, dicta
una verdad como un soplo.
Después del amor, la tierra.
Después de la tierra, todo.

72

El número de sangres
que el mundo iluminó
en dos halló el principio:
tú y yo.

El número de sangres
que es cada vez mayor
en dos busca sus fines:
tú y yo.

El número de sangres
que en el espacio son
en dos son infinitos:
tú y yo.

of raised and bristling
hair that I display.

Dry winds will not
parch the oozy seas.
And the heart stays fresh
in its August gaol
under the voice's spell,
gentlest way of streams:

'Miguel, I remember you
when sun and dust are spent,
ahead of the very moon,
tomb of love's sleep.'

Love, save me from
my former ruin,
and building me back up, utter
some breathlike truth.
After love, the earth.
After the earth, all.

72

The number of bloods
that the world lit up
flowed out in two:
you and I.

The number of bloods
that is greater each time
will stay in two:
you and I.

The number of bloods
that I carry around
poured out in two:
you and I.

73

La cantidad de mundos
que con los ojos abres,
que cierras con los brazos.

La cantidad de mundos
que con los ojos cierras,
que con los brazos abres.

74

Entre nuestras dos sangres
algo que aparta, algo
que aleja, impide, ciega,
sucede, palmo a palmo.

Entre nuestras dos sangres
va sucediendo algo,
arraiga el horizonte,
hace anchura el espacio.
Entre nuestras dos sangres
ha de suceder algo,
un puente como un niño,
un niño como un arco.

Entre nuestras dos sangres
hay cárceles con manos.
Cuanto sucede queda
entre los dos de paso.

73

The amount of worlds
you open with your eyes
and close with your arms.

The amount of worlds
you close with your eyes
and open with your arms.

74

Between our two bloods,
by inches, something happens
that removes, something that
distances, hinders, blinds.

Between our two bloods
something finally happens;
it roots the horizon,
turns space into width.
Between our two bloods
something must happen,
a bridge like a child,
a child like an arch.

Between our two bloods
there are prisons with hands.
Whatever happens stays
in passing, between us two.

75

A la luna venidera
te acostarás a parir
y tu vientre irradiará
claridades sobre mí.

Alborada de tu vientre,
cada vez más claro en sí,
esclareciendo los pozos,
anocheciendo el marfil.

A la luna venidera
el mundo se vuelve a abrir.

76

Vino. Dejó las armas,
las garras, la maleza.

La suavidad que sube,
la suavidad que reina
sobre la voz, el paso,
sobre la piel, la pierna,
arrebató su cuerpo
y estremeció sus cuerdas.

Se consumó la fiera.

La noche sobrehumana
la sangre ungió de estrellas,
relámpagos, caricias,
silencios,
besos, penas.

Memoria de la fiera.

Pero al venir el alba
se abalanzó sobre ella

75

At the next moon
you will go into labour
and your womb will cast
clarity on me.

Your womb's dawning
itself ever clearer
illuminating wells,
benighting ivory.

At the next moon
the world opens again.

76

He arrived. He left his weapons,
his claws, his thistles.

Gentleness that rises,
gentleness that rules
over the voice, the step,
over the skin, the leg,
overtook his body,
and shook his cords.

The wild beast was sealed.

The superhuman night
anointed blood with stars,
lightnings, caresses,
hushes,
kisses, griefs.

Memory of the wild beast.

But with the coming of dawn
he jumped on it

y recobró las armas,
las garras, la maleza.
Salió. Se fue dejando
locas de amor las puertas.

Se reanimó la fiera.
Y espera desde entonces
hasta que el hombre vuelva.

77

El mundo es como aparece
ante mis cinco sentidos,
y ante los tuyos que son
las orillas de los míos.
El mundo de los demás
no es el nuestro: no es el mismo.
Lecho del agua que soy,
tú, los dos, somos el río
donde cuanto más profundo
se ve más despacio y límpido.
Imágenes de la vida:
cada vez las recibimos,
nos reciben entregados
más unidamente a un ritmo.
Pero las cosas se forman
con nuestros propios delirios.
El aire tiene el tamaño
del corazón que respiro
y el sol es como la luz
con que yo le desafío.
Ciegos para los demás,
oscuros, siempre remisos,
miramos siempre hacia adentro,
vemos desde lo más íntimo.
Trabajo y amor me cuesta
conmigo así, ver contigo;
aparecer, como el agua
con la arena, siempre unidos.

and retrieved his weapons,
his claws, his thistles.
He left. He went away
leaving doors love-struck.

The wild beast recovered.
And it waits ever since
until man will return.

77

The world is what
meets my five senses
and yours that are
the shores of mine.
The world of others
is not our world: not the same.
I am the riverbed,
you, we, the river
which at its deepest
looks slowest and clearest.
Images of life:
they receive us,
as we receive them,
in ever greater unison.
But things are made
of our own ravings.
Air is the size
of the heart I breathe
and a rival light in me
challenges the sun.
Blind to others,
dark, always remiss,
we look ever inward,
gaze from the inmost.
I work and love lays me
so, to see you.
As I am, like water
and sand, always at one.

Nadie me verá del todo
ni es nadie como lo miro.
Somos algo más que vemos,
algo menos que inquirimos.
Algún suceso de todos
pasa desapercibido.
Nadie nos ha visto. A nadie
ciegos de ver, hemos visto.

78

GUERRA

Todas las madres del mundo
ocultan el vientre, tiemblan,
y quisieran retirarse
a virginidades ciegas,
el origen solitario
y el pasado sin herencia.
Pálida, sobrecogida
la fecundidad se queda.
El mar tiene sed y tiene
sed de ser agua la tierra.

Alarga la llama el odio
y el amor cierra las puertas.
Voces como lanzas vibran,
voces como bayonetas.
Bocas como puños vienen,
puños como cascos llegan.
Pechos como muros roncos,
piernas como patas recias.
El corazón se revuelve,
se atorbellina, revienta.
Arroja contra los ojos
súbitas espumas negras.

La sangre enarbola el cuerpo,
precipita la cabeza

No one sees me in my totality,
nor I another.
We are rather more than we see,
rather less than we seek.
Something that concerns us all
passes unnoticed.
No one has seen us. Blinded
by sheer sight, we've seen no one.

78

WAR

All the mothers of the world
hide their womb, tremble,
and would retreat
to blind virginities,
to a solitary source
and to a past without heritage.
Pale, shocked,
their fertility remains.
The sea is thirsty and earth
thirsts to become water.

Hatred fuels the flame,
and love slams all doors.
Voices like lances twang,
voices like bayonets.
Mouths as fists come,
fists like hooves arrive.
Chests like raucous walls,
animal-tough legs.
The heart pounds,
spins, explodes.
Against the eyes it flings
sudden black foam.

Blood raises the body,
hurls the head,

y busca un hueco, una herida
por donde lanzarse afuera.

La sangre recorre el mundo
enjaulada, insatisfecha.
Las flores se desvanecen
devoradas por la hierba.
Ansias de matar invaden
el fondo de la azucena.
Acoplarse con metales
todos los cuerpos anhelan:
desposarse, poseerse
de una terrible manera.

Desaparecer: el ansia
general, creciente, reina.
Un fantasma de estandartes,
una bandera quimérica,
un mito de patrias: una
grave ficción de fronteras.

Músicas exasperadas,
duras como botas, huellan
la faz de las esperanzas
y de las entrañas tiernas.
Crepita el alma, la ira.
El llanto relampaguea.
¿Para qué quiero la luz
si tropiezo con tinieblas?

Pasiones como clarines,
coplas, trompas que aconsejan
devorarse ser a ser,
destruirse, piedra a piedra.
Relinchos. Retumbos. Truenos.
Salivazos. Besos. Ruedas.
Espuelas. Espadas locas
abren una herida inmensa.

and seeks a gap, a wound
to emerge through.

Blood courses the world,
caged, unsatisfied.
Flowers disappear
devoured by grass.
A yearning to kill invades
the heart of the lily.
All bodies sigh
to couple with metals,
to wed, to possess each other
in a terrible manner.

To vanish: a common
longing grows, holds sway ...
A phantom banner,
a chimerical flag,
a myth of fatherlands, a
serious fiction of frontiers.

Exasperated musics,
hard as boots, tread
the face of hopes
and of tender entrails.
The soul crackles in wrath.
Weeping flashes up.
Of what use is light to me
if I bump against darkness?

Passions like bugles,
tunes, trumpets that commend
a mutual devouring,
destruction, stone by stone.
Neighing. Pounding. Thunder.
Spitting. Kisses. Wheels.
Spurs. Frenzied swords
open a vast wound.

Después, el silencio, mudo
de algodón, blanco de vendas,
cárdeno de cirugía,
mutilado de tristeza.
El silencio. Y el laurel
en un rincón de osamentas.
Y un tambor enamorado,
como un vientre tenso, suena
detrás del innumerable
muerto que jamás se aleja.

79

NANAS DE LA CEBOLLA

La cebolla es escarcha
cerrada y pobre:
escarcha de tus días
y de mis noches.
Hambre y cebolla:
hielo negro y escarcha
grande y redonda.

En la cuna del hambre
mi niño estaba.
Con sangre de cebolla
se amamantaba.
Pero tu sangre,
escarchaba de azúcar,
cebolla y hambre.

Una mujer morena,
resuelta en luna,
se derrama hilo a hilo
sobre la cuna.
Ríete, niño,
que te tragas la luna
cuando es preciso.

Then silence, mute
like cotton, white like bandages,
livid with surgery,
crippled with sadness.
Silence. And the laurel tree
over a charnel house.
And a love-sick drum,
like a tense womb, sounds
behind the innumerable
dead that won't go away.

79

LULLABIES OF THE ONION

The onion is hoarfrost,
hard and poor,
hoarfrost of your days
and of my nights.
Hunger and onion;
black ice and hoarfrost
large and round.

My child lay
in a cot of hunger;
he was fed
onion blood.
But blood from you:
sugar syrup,
onion and hunger.

A dusky woman,
melting in moonlight,
falls on the cot
in trickling threads.
Laugh, child,
for you swallow the moon
if you must.

Alondra de mi casa,
ríete mucho.
Es tu risa en los ojos
la luz del mundo.
Ríete tanto
que en el alma, al oírte,
bata el espacio.

Tu risa me hace libre,
me pone alas.
Soledades me quita,
cárcel me arranca.
Boca que vuela,
corazón que en tus labios
relampaguea.

Es tu risa la espada
más victoriosa.
Vencedor de las flores
y las alondras.
Rival del sol,
porvenir de mis huesos
y de mi amor.

La carne aleteante,
súbito el párpado,
y el niño como nunca
coloreado.
¡Cuánto jilguero
se remonta, aletea,
desde tu cuerpo!

Desperté de ser niño.
Nunca despiertes.
Triste llevo la boca.
Ríete siempre.
Siempre en la cuna,
defendiendo la risa
pluma por pluma.

Lark of my house,
laugh with delight.
Your smiling eyes
are the world's light.
Laugh until
space hears and
throbs in the soul.

Your chortle frees me,
gives me wings,
dispels my solitude,
pulls down my prison.
Sprightly mouth,
zigzagging heart
on your lips.

Your laughter,
victor among flowers
and larks,
a sword most triumphant,
rival sun.
My bones' prospect
and my love's.

The flesh aflutter,
the eyelid sudden,
never ever
so bright a child.
How many linnets
soar and flutter
off your body!

I awoke from childhood:
may you never awake.
Mine is a sad mouth:
may you laugh always.
In your cot
guard always
laughter's every feather.

Ser de vuelo tan alto,
tan extendido,
que tu carne parece
cielo cernido.
¡Si yo pudiera
remontarme al origen
de tu carrera!

Al octavo mes ríes
con cinco azahares.
Con cinco diminutas
ferocidades.
Con cinco dientes
como cinco jazmines
adolescentes.

Frontera de los besos
serán mañana,
cuando en la dentadura
sientas un arma.
Sientas un fuego
correr dientes abajo
buscando el centro.

Vuela niño en la doble
luna del pecho.
Él, triste de cebolla.
Tú, satisfecho.
No te derrumbes.
No sepas lo que pasa
ni lo que ocurre.

Soar so high,
so far,
your flesh is heaven
just born.
Could I but
soar again
to your flight's start!

Eight months and you smile
with five orange blossoms.
With five tiny
ferocities.
With five teeth
like five young
jasmines.

Tomorrow they'll be
the boundary of kisses,
and you'll feel a weapon
in their edge,
a flame
they'll send
biting your very marrow.

Never, child, up
in the twin-moon breast:
it, sad, with onion,
you, contented.
Don't fall.
Ignore what happens
or what goes on.

B

CANCIONERO DE AUSENCIAS

80

Debajo del granado
de mi pasión
amor, amor he llorado
¡ay de mi corazón!

Al fondo del granado
de mi pasión
el fruto se ha desangrado
¡ay de mi corazón!

81

El mar también elige
puertos donde reír
como los marineros.

El mar de los que son.

El mar también elige
puertos donde morir.
Como los marineros.

El mar de los que fueron.

B

SONGBOOK OF ABSENCES

80

Under the pomegranate tree
of my passion
love, love I have wept
Ah, for my heart!

Behind the pomegranate tree
of my passion
the fruit has been bled white
Ah, for my heart!

81

The sea, too, chooses
ports to laugh in
as do sailors.

The sea of the living.

The sea, too, chooses
ports to die in.
As do sailors.

The sea of the departed.

82

¿Quién llenará este vacío
de cielo desalentado
que deja tu cuerpo al mío?

83

No vale entristecerse.
La sombra que te lo ha dado.
La sombra que se lo lleve.

84

Me descansa
sentir que te arrullan
las aguas.
Me consuela
sentir que te abraza
la tierra.

85

Cuerpos, soles, alboradas,
cárceles y cementerios,
donde siempre hay un pedazo
de sombra para mi cuerpo.

82

Who will fill up
this disheartened body-space
your body left mine?

83

Not worth brooding.
Let the shadow it has given you
carry it off and away too.

84

It relieves me
to feel a stream
lullabying you.
It comforts me
to feel earth
hugging you.

85

Bodies, suns, dawns,
prisons and graveyards
in which there's always a patch
of shade for my body.

86

Suave aliento suave
claro cuerpo claro
densa frente densa
penetrante labio.
Vida caudalosa,
vientre de dos arcos.
Todo lo he perdido, tierra
todo lo has ganado

87

Los animales íntimos
que forman tu pasado
hicieron firme la negrura de tu pelo.
Los animales íntimos
que forman mi pasado
ambicionaron con firmeza retenerlo.

88

Enciende las dos puertas,
abre la lumbre.
No sé lo que me pasa
que tropiezo en las nubes.

89

Entre las fatalidades
que somos tú y yo, él ha sido
la fatalidad más grande.

86

Soft breath soft
clear body clear
dense forehead dense
thrusting lip.
Surging life,
twin arch belly.
I have lost it all, earth
you have won it all.

87

The intimate animals
that form your past
gave firmness to the blackness of your hair.
The intimate animals
that form my past
had the firm ambition to retain it.

88

Light up the two doors,
open the hearth.
I don't know what ails me
that I stumble on clouds.

89

Ill-fated though we are, you and I,
he has been
ill-fated most of all.

90

Dicen que parezco otro.
Pero sigo siendo el mismo
desde tu vientre remoto.

91

El pozo y la palmera
se ahondan en tu cuerpo
poblado de ascendencias.

92

La oliva y el limón
las desentrañaron
desde tu corazón.

93

Tengo celos de un muerto,
de un vivo, no.

Tengo celos de un muerto
que nunca te miró.

94

Quise despedirme más,
y sólo vi tu pañuelo
lejano irse.

Imposible.

Y un golpe de polvo vino
a cegarme, ahogarme, herirme.
Polvo desde entonces trago.

Imposible.

90

They say I seem another,
but I keep being the same,
at a remove, out of your womb.

91

The well and the palm-tree
are sunk in your body
peopled with ascendencies.

92

The olive and the lemon
were unbosomed
from within your heart.

93

I am jealous of someone dead,
not someone living.

I am jealous of someone dead
who never saw you.

94

I wanted to wave still
and I saw just your distant
handkerchief disappear.

Impossible.

And a blast of dust blew up
and blinded, choked, hurt me.
I swallow dust since then.

Impossible.

95

No te asomes
a la ventana,
que no hay nada en esta casa.

Asómate a mi alma.

No te asomes
al cementerio,
que no hay nada entre estos huesos.

Asómate a mi cuerpo.

96

De la contemplación
nace la rosa:
del amor el naranjo
y el laurel:
tú y yo del beso aquél.

97

Muerto mío.
Te has ido con el verano.
¿Sientes frío?

95

Don't look
through the window;
there's nothing in this house.

Look into my soul.

Don't look
into the cemetery;
there's nothing among those bones.

Look into my body.

96

From contemplation
the rose is born;
from contemplation
the orange and the bay tree.
You and I from a kiss.

97

My dead one.
You have left along with summer.
Are you feeling cold?

98

Dime desde allá abajo
la palabra *te quiero*.

¿Hablas bajo la tierra?

Hablo como el silencio.

¿Quieres bajo la tierra?

Bajo la tierra quiero
porque hacia donde cruzas
quiere cruzar mi cuerpo.

Ardo desde allá abajo
y alumbro tu recuerdo.

99

Querer, querer, querer:
ésa fue mi corona,
ésa es.

100

Ni te lavas ni te peinas,
ni sales de ese rincón.
Contigo puede la sombra,
conmigo el sol.

98

Tell me, from there below,
the words *I love you*.

Do you speak, under the earth?

I speak like silence.

Do you love, under the earth?

I love, under the earth,
because wherever you will go
my body longs to follow.

I burn from there below
and bring to light your memories.

99

To love, love, love:
that was my crown.
And there it is.

100

You won't wash or comb
or leave that nook of yours.
Shadow falls to you;
to me, sunlight.

101

Llama, ¿para quién?
Llama, para alguien.
Cruza las tinieblas
y no alumbra a nadie.

102

Son míos, ¡ay! son míos
los bellos cuerpos muertos,
los bellos cuerpos vivos,
los cuerpos venideros.

Son míos, ¡ay! son míos
a través de tu cuerpo.

103

Tanto río que va al mar
donde no hace falta el agua.
Tantos campos que se secan.
Tantos cuerpos que se abrazan.

104

La fuerza que me arrastra
hacia el sur de la tierra
es mi sangre primera.

La fuerza que me arrastra
hacia el fondo del sur,
muerto mío, eres tú.

101

Flame, for whom?
Flame, for someone.
It shoots the dark through
and it brings light to no one.

102

Ah, they are mine. Mine,
the beautiful dead bodies,
the beautiful living bodies,
the bodies to be.

Ah, they are mine. Mine,
through your body.

103

So many rivers bound for the sea,
to abundant waters.
So many dried-up bodies.
So many bodies locked in embrace.

104

The force that pulls me
to the south of the earth
is my pristine blood.

The force that pulls me
to the depth of the south,
my dear dead child, is you.

105

Cuando te hablo del muerto
se te quedan las manos
quietas sobre mi cuerpo.

Háblame de la muerta.
Y encontrarás mis manos
sobre tu cuerpo quietas.

106

No puedo olvidar
que no tengo alas,
que no tengo mar,
vereda ni nada
con que irte a besar.

107

¿Para qué me has parido, mujer?:
¿para qué me has parido?

Para dar a los cuerpos de allá
este cuerpo que siento hacia aquí,
hacia ti traído.

Para qué me has parido, mujer,
si tan lejos de ti me has parido.

108

Tú de blanco, yo de negro,
vestidos nos abrazamos.
Vestidos aunque desnudos
tú de negro, yo de blanco.

105

When I tell you about him, the dead one,
your hands stand
still upon my body.

Speak to me of the dead one.
And you will find my hands
tranquil on your body.

106

I cannot forget
I have no wings,
I have no sea,
no path or way
to go and kiss you.

107

What use giving birth to me, woman?
What use giving birth to me?

So you'd give to the bodies beyond
this body I feel tied here,
dragged towards you.

What use giving birth to me, woman,
when you bore me so faraway from you?

108

We embrace, dressed,
you in white, I in black.
Dressed though naked
you in black, I in white.

109

De aquel querer mío,
¿qué queda en el aire?

Sólo un traje frío
donde ardió la sangre.

110

Rotos, rotos: ¡Qué rotos!
Rotos: cristales rotos
de tanto dilatarse
en ver, arder, querer,
luchar, odiar, mis ojos.

Rotos: por siempre rotos.
Rotos: espejos rotos
caídos, sin imagen,
sin dirección, tus ojos.

C

OTROS POEMAS DEL CICLO (I)

111

Qué cara de herido pongo
cuando te veo y me miro
por la ribera del hombro.

Enterrado me veo,
crucificado
en la cruz y en el hoyo
del desengaño:
qué mala luna
me ha empujado a quererte
como a ninguna.

109

Of that love of mine
what hangs in the air?

Only a cold garment
where blood burned.

110

Broken, broken, so broken!
Broken: broken panes
with so much straining
at seeing, lighting, loving,
struggling, hating, my eyes.

Broken: forever broken.
Broken mirrors,
fallen, imageless,
aimless, your eyes.

C

OTHER POEMS OF THE CYCLE (I)

111

What a wounded man I look
when along the shoulder's slope
I see you and view myself.

I see myself buried,
crucified
on the cross and in the tomb
of disillusion.
What fateful moon
has driven me to love you
as no one else.

112

No sigas muerto
retrocede a la vida—
¿retrocede la lluvia?
¿retrocedería?

113

Pongo cara de herido
cuando respiras
y de muerto que sufre
cuando me miras.
Tú has conseguido
tenerme a cada instante
muerto y herido.

114

Cuando respiras me hieres,
cuando me miras me matas,
tus cejas son dos cuchillos
negros, tus negras pestañas.

115

Por la voz de la herida
que tú me has hecho
habla desembocando
todo mi pecho.
Es mi persona
una torre de heridas
que se desploma.

112

Don't stay dead
retreat into your life –
does rain retreat?
Would it?

113

I put on the looks of the wounded
when you breathe
and the looks of one dead that suffers
when you gaze on me.
You have managed
to keep me each instant
dead and wounded.

114

When you breathe you wound me,
when you look at me you slay me,
your eyebrows are two black
knives, your black eyelashes.

115

Through the voice of the wound
you have caused me
all my chest
empties and speaks.
All of me is
one tower of wounds
crumbling down.

116

Que me aconseje el mar
lo que tengo que hacer:
si matar, si querer.

117

EL ÚLTIMO RINCÓN

El último y el primero:
rincón para el sol más grande,
sepultura de esta vida
donde tus ojos no caben.

Allí quisiera tenderme
para desenamorarme.

Por el olivo lo quiero,
lo persigo por la calle,
se sume por los rincones
donde se sumen los árboles.

Se ahonda y hace más honda
la intensidad de mi sangre.

Los olivos moribundos
florecen en todo el aire
y los muchachos se quedan
cercanos y agonizantes.

Carne de mi movimiento,
huesos de ritmos mortales:
me muero por respirar
sobre vuestros ademanes.

116

Let the sea advise me
on what I must do;
to kill, to love.

117

THE LAST CORNER

Last and first:
a corner for the greatest sun,
a tomb of this life
where your eyes don't fit.

There I would spread out
to fall out of love.

I like it in the olive tree,
I sense it in the street,
it seeps through the corners
where trees merge.

My blood's intensity
sinks and deepens.

The dying olive trees
blossom in all the air
and the boys stay
close by and agonizing.

Flesh of my movement,
bones of mortal rhythms,
I die for breathing
high over your signals.

Corazón que entre dos piedras
ansiosas de machacarte,
de tanto querer te ahogas
como un mar entre dos mares.

De tanto querer me ahogo,
y no me es posible ahogarme.

Beso que viene rodando
desde el principio del mundo
a mi boca por tus labios.
Beso que va al porvenir,
boca como un doble astro
que entre los astros palpita
por tantos besos parados,
por tantas bocas cerradas
sin un beso solitario.

¿Qué hice para que pusieran
a mi vida tanta cárcel?

Tu pelo donde lo negro
ha sufrido las edades
de la negrura más firme,
y la más emocionante:
tu secular pelo negro
recorro hasta remontarme
a la negrura primera
de tus ojos y tus padres,
al rincón de pelo denso
donde relampagueaste.

Como un rincón solitario
allí el hombre brota y arde.

Ay, el rincón de tu vientre;
el callejón de tu carne;
el callejón sin salida
donde agonicé una tarde.

Heart between two stones
intent on crushing it,
with so much loving you drown
like a sea between two seas.

With so much loving I drown,
and I cannot drown myself.

A kiss that comes wheeling
from the beginning of the world
to my mouth for your lips.
A kiss that goes to the future,
a mouth like a double star
which pulses among the stars
for so many halted kisses,
for so many closed mouths
without a solitary kiss.

What did I do that they made
my life so much prison?

Your hair where blackness
has withstood ages
of the most enduring and
stirring blackness:
I retrace your age-old hair
till I regain
the earliest blackness
of your eyes and parents,
the hideaway of dense hair,
where your lightning flashed.

Like a solitary corner
There man erupts and glows.

Ah, your womb's hideaway,
alley-way of your flesh,
the blind alley
where one afternoon I writhed.

La pólvora y el amor
marchan sobre las ciudades
deslumbrando, removiendo
la población de la sangre.

El naranjo sabe a vida
el olivo a tiempo sabe.
Y entre el clamor de los dos
mis pasiones se debaten.

El último y el primero:
rincón donde algún cadáver
siente el arrullo del mundo
de los amorosos cauces.

Siesta que ha entenebrecido
el sol de las humedades.

Allí quisiera tenderme
para desenamorarme.

Después del amor, la tierra.
Después de la tierra, nadie.

118

CANTAR

Es la casa un palomar
y la cama un jazminero.
Las puertas de par en par
y en el fondo el mundo entero.

El hijo, tu corazón
madre que se ha engrandecido.
Dentro de la habitación
todo lo que ha florecido.
El hijo te hace un jardín,
y tú has hecho al hijo, esposa,

Powder and love
march on cities
with glare and convulsion
to people and blood.

The orange tree tastes of life
and the olive tree tastes of time,
and between the clamour of the two
my heart is in conflict.

Last and first:
shipwrecked corner, dam
of slaver held
up its amorous bed.

Siesta that has darkened
the moistened sun.

I would spread out there
to fall out of love.

After love, the earth.
After the earth, no one.

118

SONG

The house is a dovecote
and the bed a jasmine bush.
Doors wide open
and, far back, all the world.

The son, mother,
your heart grown large.
Within the room,
all that ever bloomed.
The son makes you a garden,
wife, and you have made the son

la habitación del jazmín,
el palomar de la rosa.

Alrededor de tu piel
ato y desato la mía.
Un mediodía de miel
rezumas: un mediodía.

¿Quién en esta casa entró
y la apartó del desierto?
Para que me acuerde yo,
alguien que soy yo y ha muerto.

Viene la luz más redonda
a los almendros más blancos.
La vida, la luz se ahonda
entre muertos y barrancos.

Venturoso es el futuro,
como aquellos horizontes
de pórfido y mármol puro
donde respiran los montes.

Arde la casa encendida
de besos y sombra amante.
No puede pasar la vida
más honda y emocionante.

Desbordadamente sorda
la leche alumbra tus huesos.
Y la casa se desborda
con ella, el hijo y los besos.

Tú, tu vientre caudaloso,
el hijo y el palomar.
Esposa, sobre tu esposo
suenan los pasos del mar.

the jasmine's chamber
and the rose's dovecote.

All round your skin
I bind and unbind mine.
Noon as honey, a noon
oozes out of you.

Who entered this house
and cut it off the desert?
For me to remember
the man I am, a dead man.

The starkest light comes
to the whitest almond trees.
Life, light, is deepened
with the dead and the ravines.

The future is fortunate
as those horizons
of porphyry and pure marble
where the mountains breathe.

Aflame, the house burns
with kisses and loving shade.
Life could not go by
deeper and more moving.

The milkflow, rich to deafness,
drains you to the bone.
And the house brims over
with it, the son and kisses.

You, your bounteous womb,
the son and the dovecote.
Over your husband, wife,
the treading sea beats.

119

El pez más viejo del río
de tanta sabiduría
como amontonó, vivía
brillantemente sombrío.
Y el agua le sonreía.

Tan sombrío llegó a estar
(nada el agua le divierte)
que después de meditar,
tomó el camino del mar,
es decir, el de la muerte.

Reíste tú junto al río,
niño solar. Y ese día
el pez más viejo del río
se quitó el aire sombrío.
Y el agua te sonreía.

120

Rueda que irás muy lejos.
Ala que irás muy alto.
Torre del día, niño.
Alborear del pájaro.
Niño: ala, rueda, torre.
Pie. Pluma. Espuma. Rayo.
Ser como nunca ser.
Nunca serás en tanto.

Eres mañana. Ven
con todo de la mano.
Eres mi ser que vuelve
hacia su ser más claro.
El universo eres
que guía esperanzado.

119

The oldest fish of the river
lived in brilliant gloom
thanks to the vast wisdom
he had amassed.
And the water smiled at him.

He became so gloomy
(no longer amused by water)
that after meditating
he took the route to the sea,
that is, the way to death.

You laughed, solar child,
by the river. And that day
the oldest fish of the river
shed his gloomy air.
And the water smiled at you.

120

A wheel, you'll go quite far.
A wing, you'll fly quite high.
Child, towering day,
a bird's sunrise.
Child: wing, wheel, tower.
Foot, feather, foam, flash.
Being as none is to be.
You'll never again be such.

You are tomorrow. Yet,
come led by the hand.
You are my own being brought
back to its purest self.
You are the universe
that leads, in hope.

Pasión del movimiento,
la tierra es tu caballo.
Cabálgala. Domínala.
Y brotará en su casco
su piel de vida y muerte,
de sombra y luz, piafando.
Asciende. Rueda. Vuela,
creador de alba y mayo.
Galopa. Ven. Y colma
el fondo de mis brazos.

121

Con dos años, dos flores
cumples ahora.
Dos alondras llenando
toda tu aurora.
Niño radiante:
va mi sangre contigo
siempre adelante.

Sangre mía, adelante,
no retrocedas.
La luz rueda en el mundo,
mientras tú ruedas.
Todo te mueve,
universo de un cuerpo
dorado y leve.

Herramienta es tu risa,
luz que proclama
la victoria del trigo
sobre la grama.
Ríe. Contigo
venceré siempre al tiempo
que es mi enemigo.

Passion of movement,
the earth is your horse.
Ride it. Command it.
Its shell will sprout
a hide of life and death,
of shadow and light, stomping.
Rise. Roll. Fly,
maker of dawn and May.
Gallop. Come. And fill
the hollow of my arms.

121

With your two years, you now
attain two flowers.
Two larks filling
all of your dawn.
Radiant child;
my blood moves with you
ever forward.

Blood of mine, advance,
do not retreat.
Light rolls in the world
while you roll.
All things propel you,
universe of a light
and golden body.

Your laughter is tools,
a light that proclaims
the victory of wheat
over grass.
Laugh. With you
I'll always conquer time
that is my enemy.

122

CASIDA DEL SEDIENTO

Arena del desierto
soy: desierto de sed.
Oasis es tu boca
donde no he de beber.

Boca: oasis abierto
a todas las arenas del desierto.

Húmedo punto en medio
de un mundo abrasador,
el de tu cuerpo, el tuyo,
que nunca es de los dos.

Cuerpo: pozo cerrado
a quien la sed y el sol han calcinado.

Ocaña, mayo, 1941

123

Desenterrar vivos.
Yo avivar
tú parir muertos
eso haces mujer
cuando te acuestas.
Eso hacemos.

124

Todo es bueno
y lo hacemos malo
con nuestro veneno.

122

CASIDA OF THIRST

I am desert sand:
a desert of thirst.
Your mouth is an oasis
where I may not drink.

Mouth: an oasis open
to all the desert's sand.

In a scorching world
a moist spot:
your body's, yours,
and never of us two.

Body: a well closed
to one parched with thirst and sun.

Ocaña, May, 1941

123

Exhuming the living.
I, quicken the dead,
you bring them forth;
that's what you do, woman,
when you lie in bed.
That's what we both do.

124

Everything is good
and we make it bad
with our poison.

125

Conozco bien los caminos
conozco los caminantes
del mar, del fuego, del sueño,
de la tierra, de los aires.
Y te conozco a ti
que estás dentro de mi sangre.

126

Písame,
que ya no me quejo.

Ódiame,
que ya no lo siento.

No me olvides
que aún te recuerdo
debajo del plomo
que embarga mis huesos.

125

I know the routes well
I know the travellers
of the sea, of fire, sleep,
earth, air.
And I know you
who are inside my blood.

126

Tread on me,
for I no longer complain.

Loathe me,
for I no longer feel it.

Don't forget me
for under the lead
that pins my bones
I still remember you.

D

OTROS POEMAS DEL CICLO (II)

127

TODO ERA AZUL

Todo era azul delante de aquellos ojos y era
verde hasta lo entrañable, dorado hasta muy lejos.
Porque el color hallaba su encarnación primera
dentro de aquellos ojos de frágiles reflejos.

Ojos nacientes: luces en una doble esfera.
Todo radiaba en torno como un solar de espejos.
Vivificar las cosas para la primavera
poder fue de unos ojos que nunca han sido viejos.

Se los devoran. ¿Sabes? No soy feliz. No hay goce
como sentir aquella mirada inundadora.
Cuando se me alejaba, me despedí del día.

La claridad brotaba de su directo roce,
pero los devoraron. Y están brotando ahora
penumbras como el pardo rubor de la agonía.

128

SONREÍR CON LA ALEGRE
TRISTEZA DEL OLIVO

Sonreír con la alegre tristeza del olivo.
Esperar. No cansarse de esperar la alegría.
Sonriamos. Doremos la luz de cada día
en esta alegre y triste vanidad del ser vivo.

Me siento cada día más libre y más cautivo
en toda esta sonrisa tan clara y tan sombría.
Cruzan las tempestades sobre tu boca fría
como sobre la mía que aún es un soplo estivo.

D

OTHER POEMS OF THE CYCLE (II)

127

EVERYTHING WAS BLUE

Before those eyes all was blue
and green to the intimate, to the farthest gilt.
For in those eyes of frail sparkles
colour found its first embodiment.

Rising eyes: lights in twin spheres.
All around, it beamed as a sun-lit plot of mirrors.
It was the power of eyes that never aged,
to enliven things for the springtime.

They're being devoured. Don't you know? I am not happy.
There's no joy like feeling that flooding look.
When it moved off me, I parted with daylight.

Out of their straight touch brightness flashed,
but they were devoured. And now twilights are seeping
as gray as the shame of the death-throes.

128

SMILING WITH THE HAPPY
SADNESS OF THE OLIVE TREE

To smile with the sad joy of the olive tree.
To wait. Not to tire of waiting for joy.
Let's smile. Let's gild the light of each day
with this vanity, both happy and sad, of living things.

Each day I feel both freer and more captive
amid all this smiling so clear and so sombre.
Storms glide over your cold mouth
as they do over mine where summer still breathes faintly.

Una sonrisa se alza sobre el abismo: crece
como un abismo trémulo, pero valiente en alas.
Una sonrisa eleva calientemente el vuelo.

Diurna, firme, arriba, no baja, no anochece.
Todo lo desafías, amor: todo lo escalas.
Con sonrisa te fuiste de la tierra y del cielo.

129

YO NO QUIERO MÁS LUZ QUE
TU CUERPO ANTE EL MÍO

Yo no quiero más luz que tu cuerpo ante el mío:
claridad absoluta, transparencia redonda.
Limpidez cuya extraña, como el fondo del río,
con el tiempo se afirma, con la sangre se ahonda.

¿Qué lucientes materias duraderas te han hecho,
corazón de alborada, carnación matutina?
Yo no quiero más día que el que exhala tu pecho.
Tu sangre es la mañana que jamás se termina.

No hay más luz que tu cuerpo, no hay más sol: todo ocaso.
Yo no veo las cosas a otra luz que tu frente.
La otra luz es fantasma, nada más, de tu paso.
Tu insondable mirada nunca gira al poniente.

Claridad sin posible declinar. Suma esencia
del fulgor que ni cede ni abandona la cumbre.
Juventud. Limpidez. Claridad. Transparencia
acercando los astros más lejanos de lumbre.

Claro cuerpo moreno de calor fecundante.
Hierba negra el origen; hierba negra las sienes.
Trago negro los ojos, la mirada distante.
Día azul. Noche clara. Sombra clara que vienes.

Yo no quiero más luz que tu sombra dorada
donde brotan anillos de una hierba sombría.
En mi sangre, fielmente por tu cuerpo abrasada,
para siempre es de noche: para siempre es de día.

Above the abyss a smile rises; it grows
as would a tremulous but brave-winged abyss.
Warmly, a smile raises its flight.

Diurnal, firm, upward, it won't descend, there's no nightfall.
Love, you defy all, climb up everything.
With a smile you left both earth and heaven.

129

I WANT NO MORE LIGHT THAN
YOUR BODY FACING MINE

I want no more light than your body facing mine:
absolute brightness, round transparency.
A limpidity whose innards, like a river's bed,
time makes the greater and blood the deeper.

What shining, durable stuffs have shaped you,
daybreak heart, sunrise complexion?
I want that light your breast throws, no other.
Your blood is a morning that will not elapse.

There's no light besides your body, no sun: all sunset.
I see things by no light other than your front.
Another light is but the phantom of you moving past.
Unfathomable, your gaze never turns westwards.

Brightness that could not wane. Utmost essence
of a brilliance that won't relent or leave the summit.
Youth. Limpidity. Clarity. Transparency
that brings closer stars shining farthest off.

Bright, swarthy body, fruitfully warm.
At its base as on its temples black grass.
The eyes a black gulp, remote look.
Blue daytime. Clear night. Clear shade approaching.

I want no other light than your golden shade
in which sombre, grassy ringlets sprout.
In my blood, that faithfully your body has set ablaze,
all is forever night, all is forever day.

130
19 DE DICIEMBRE DE 1937

Desde que el alba quiso ser alba, toda eres
madre. Quiso la luna profundamente llena.
En tu dolor lunar he visto dos mujeres,
y un removido abismo bajo una luz serena.

¡Qué olor de madreselva desgarrada y hendida!
¡Qué exaltación de labios y honduras generosas!
Bajo las huecas ropas aleteó la vida,
y se sintieron vivas bruscamente las cosas.

Eres más clara. Eres más tierna. Eres más suave.
Ardes y te consumes con más recogimiento.
El nuevo amor te inspira la levedad del ave
y ocupa los caminos pausados de tu aliento.

Ríe, porque eres madre con luna. Así lo expresa
tu palidez rendida de recorrer lo rojo;
y ese cerezo exhausto que en tu corazón pesa,
y el ascua repentina que te agiganta el ojo.

Ríe, que todo ríe: que todo es madre leve.
Profundidad del mundo sobre el que te has quedado
sumiéndote y ahondándote mientras la luna mueve,
igual que tú, su hermosa cabeza hacia otro lado.

Nunca tan parecida tu frente al primer cielo.
Todo lo abres, todo lo alegras, madre, aurora.
Vienen rodando el hijo y el sol. Arcos de anhelo
te impulsan. Eres madre. Sonríe. Ríe. Llora.

130

DECEMBER 19, 1937

Since dawn would be dawn you are all
mother. A deep full moon would have you be.
I have seen two women in your lunar pangs,
and an abyss astir under a placid light.

What an aroma of honeysuckle torn and cleft!
That strain of lips and bounteous depths!
Life's wings beat under the fluffy clothes,
and all things felt briskly alive.

You are clearer, more tender. You are softer.
You burn out and are spent in greater recollection.
This novel love breathes into you bird-lightness,
and fills the leisured roads of your breath.

Laugh, for you are a moonlit mother. So tells
the paleness that bestreaks the red,
and that loaded cherry-tree weighing down your heart,
and the sudden flare that gives you a giant eye.

Laugh, for everything laughs: all is weightless mother.
You hang above the world's depths,
diving and sinking while, like yourself,
the moon's lovely head turns to the other side.

Never so like the first heaven your forehead.
Mother, dawn, you open, gladden all things.
Both son and sun come rolling our way. Yearning's
arches propel you. You are mother. Smile. Laugh.

131

MUERTE NUPCIAL

El lecho, aquella hierba de ayer y de mañana:
este lienzo de ahora sobre madera aún verde,
flota como la tierra, se sume en la besana
donde el deseo encuentra los ojos y los pierde.

Pasar por unos ojos como por un desierto:
como por dos ciudades que ni un amor contienen.
Mirada que va y vuelve sin haber descubierto
el corazón a nadie, que todos la enarenen.

Mis ojos encontraron en un rincón los tuyos.
Se descubrieron mudos entre las dos miradas.
Sentimos recorrernos un palomar de arrullos,
y un golpe de arrebatos de alas arrebatadas.

Cuanto más se miraban más se hallaban: más hondos
se veían, más lejos, y más en uno fundidos.
El corazón se puso, y el mundo, más redondos.
Atravesaba el lecho la patria de los nidos.

Entonces, el anhelo creciente, la distancia
que va de hueso a hueso recorrida y unida,
al aspirar del todo la imperiosa fragancia,
proyectamos los cuerpos más allá de la vida.

Espiramos del todo. ¡Qué absoluto portento!
¡Qué total fue la dicha de mirarse abrazados,
desplegados los ojos hacia arriba un momento,
y al momento hacia abajo con los ojos plegados!

Pero no moriremos. Fue tan cálidamente
consumada la vida como el sol, su mirada.
No es posible perdernos. Somos plena simiente.
Y la muerte ha quedado, con los dos, fecundada.

131

NUPTIAL DEATH

The bed, that grass of yesterday and of tomorrow:
this present sheet upon wood still green
floats like earth, merges with the ploughland
in which desire finds and loses its eyes.

To traverse someone's eyes as one would a desert:
as one would two cities empty of all love.
The sand should cloud a look that comes and goes
not having disclosed the heart to anyone.

My eyes met yours in a nook.
Between our looks our mute eyes found each other.
We felt going over us a dovecote's cooing
and wings' flurry of fluttering flaps.

The more they looked, the more they found,
saw the deeper, the wider, each other, the greater their blend.
Both the heart and the world became rounder.
The homeland of nests cut across the bed.

Then increase of yearning, the stretch
from one's bones to the other's traversed and cancelled,
as we fully inhaled the imperious fragrance,
we fired both bodies beyond life.

We wholly exhaled. What an absolute portent!
How total the bliss of feeling embraced,
the eyes unfolding upwards for a moment,
and at once downwards, eyes folding.

But we shall not die. Life was consummated
with a sun's heat, a sun's look.
It cannot be we are lost. We are full seed.
Death has been seeded with us both.

132

EL NIÑO DE LA NOCHE

Riéndose, burlándose con claridad del día,
se hundió en la noche el niño que quise ser dos veces.
No quise más la luz. ¿Para qué? No saldría
más de aquellos silencios y aquellas lobregueces.

Quise ser... ¿Para qué?... Quise llegar gozoso
al centro de la esfera de todo lo que existe.
Quise llevar la risa como lo más hermoso.
He muerto sonriendo serenamente triste.

Niño dos veces niño: tres veces venidero.
Vuelve a rodar por ese mundo opaco del vientre.
Atrás, amor. Atrás, niño, porque no quiero
salir donde la luz su gran tristeza encuentre.

Regreso al aire plástico que alentó mi inconsciencia.
Vuelvo a rodar, consciente del sueño que me cubre.
En una sensitiva sombra de transparencia,
en un íntimo espacio rodar de octubre a octubre.

Vientre: carne central de todo lo existente.
Bóveda eternamente si azul, si roja, oscura.
Noche final en cuya profundidad se siente
la voz de las raíces y el soplo de la altura.

Bajo tu piel avanzo, y es sangre la distancia.
Mi cuerpo en una densa constelación gravita.
El universo agolpa su errante resonancia
allí, donde la historia del hombre ha sido escrita.

Mirar, y ver en torno la soledad, el monte,
el mar, por la ventana de un corazón entero
que ayer se acongojaba de no ser horizonte
abierto a un mundo menos mudable y pasajero.

132

CHILD OF THE NIGHT

Smiling, jesting with the clarity of day,
the child I wanted to be, twice, sank into the night.
I did not want the light more. Why? He would never
again leave those silences and those glooms.

I wanted to be ... Why? I wanted to reach joyful
the centre of the sphere of everything that exists.
I wanted to wear the smile like the most beautiful thing.
I have died smiling serenely sad.

Child twice child: three times coming.
He wheels again through that opaque world of the womb.
Behind, love. Behind, child, because I do not wish
to leave where the light encounters its great sadness.

I return to the plastic air which my unconscious breathed.
I wheel again, conscious of the sleep that covers me.
In a sensitive shadow of transparency,
in an intimate space to wheel from October to October.

Womb: flesh central to everything that exists.
Dome eternally dark though blue or red.
Final night in whose profundity one feels
the voice of roots and the beat of height.

Under your skin, and the distance is blood.
My body gravitates in a dense constellation.
The universe beats his errant resonance
there, where the history of man has been written.

To look, and to see the solitude, the mountain,
the sea, though the window of a complete heart
which yesterday was grieved not being a horizon
open to a world less mutable and passing.

Acumular la piedra y el niño para nada:
para vivir sin alas y oscuramente un día.
Pirámide de sal temible y limitada,
sin fuego ni frescura. No. Vuelve, vida mía.

Mas, algo me ha empujado desesperadamente.
Caigo en la madrugada del tiempo, del pasado.
Me arrojan de la noche. Y ante la luz hiriente
vuelvo a llorar, desnudo como siempre he llorado.

133

EL HOMBRE NO REPOSA...

El hombre no reposa: quien reposa es su traje
cuando, colgado, mece, su soledad con viento.
Mas, una vida incógnita como un vago tatuaje
mueve bajo las ropas dejadas un aliento.

El corazón ya cesa de ser flor de oleaje.
La frente ya no rige su potro, el firmamento.
Por más que el cuerpo, ahondando por la quietud, trabaje,
en el central reposo se cierne el movimiento.

No hay muertos. Todo vive: todo late y avanza.
Todo es un soplo extático de actividad moviente.
Piel inferior del hombre, su traje no ha expirado.

Visiblemente inmóvil, el corazón se lanza
a conmover al mundo que recorrió la frente.
Y el universo gira como un pecho pausado.

134

SIGO EN LA SOMBRA, LLENO DE LUZ: ¿EXISTE EL DÍA?

Sigo en la sombra, lleno de luz; ¿existe el día?
¿Esto es mi tumba o es mi bóveda materna?
Pasa el latido contra mi piel como una fría
losa que germinara caliente, roja, tierna.

Accumulating stone and the child for nothing:
to live a day wingless and darkly.
A pyramid of frightful and limited salt,
without fire or freshness. No. Return, life of mine.

But, something has pushed me desperately.
I fall into the morning of time, of the past.
They draw me from the night. And before the piercing light
I weep again, naked as I have always wept.

133

MAN DOES NOT REST ...

A man does not rest: it is his dress does
when, hanging, it rocks lonesome by the wind.
Then an unknown life, as if vaguely tattooed,
exhales a breath under the clothes.

Now the heart ceases to be the surf's bloom.
The forehead no longer drives its steed, the sky.
May the body so toil, burrow into stillness,
movement hovers above the resting core.

There are no dead. All is alive: all throbs and presses on.
All is one single ecstatic gust of active motion.
Man's inferior sin, his dress has not expired.

Motionless to sight, the heart undertakes
to shake the world the forehead had explored.
And the universe turns as a restful chest breathes.

134

I STAY IN THE DARK, FULL OF
LIGHT: DOES DAY EXIST?

Full of light, I stay in the dark. Does day exist?
Is this my tomb, or the maternal dome?
A heartbeat strokes my skin as would a cold
slab, could it, warm, red, tender, only bud.

Es posible que no haya nacido todavía,
o que haya muerto siempre. La sombra me gobierna.
Si esto es vivir, morir no sé yo qué sería,
ni sé lo que persigo con ansia tan eterna.

Encadenado a un traje, parece que persigo
desnudarme, librarme de aquello que no puede
ser yo y hace turbia y ausente la mirada.

Pero la tela negra, distante, va conmigo
sombra con sombra, contra la sombra hasta que ruede
a la desnuda vida creciente de la nada.

135

VUELO

Sólo quien ama vuela. Pero, ¿quién ama tanto
que sea como el pájaro más leve y fugitivo?
Hundiendo va este odio reinante todo cuanto
quisiera remontarse directamente vivo.

Amar… Pero, ¿quién ama? Volar… Pero, ¿quién vuela?
Conquistaré el azul ávido de plumaje,
pero el amor, abajo siempre, se desconsuela
de no encontrar las alas que da cierto coraje.

Un ser ardiente, claro de deseos, alado,
quiso ascender, tener la libertad por nido.
Quiso olvidar que el hombre se aleja encadenado.
Donde faltaban plumas puso valor y olvido.

Iba tan alto a veces, que le resplandecía
sobre la piel el cielo, bajo la piel el ave.
Ser que te confundiste con una alondra un día,
te desplomaste otro como el granizo grave.

It may be I have not been born yet,
or that I've died ever again. The dark rules me.
If this is to live, I don't know what to die might be.
I don't know what I seek, forever so eager.

Bound to a garb, it would seem I sought
to undress, rid myself of what cannot
be I and makes one's look dull and absent.

But the black, distant stuff comes with me,
dark with dark, to meet the dark till it shall
roll down to naked life growing from nothingness.

135

FLIGHT

Whoever loves, flies, no one else. But who loves so
as to be like the lightest, fleetest bird?
This reigning hatred is sinking all that
would soar in straight liveliness.

To love ... But who loves? To fly ... But who flies?
I shall conquer the plumage-avid blue,
but love, ever below, is disconsolate
not to find the wings a certain courage lends.

An ardent being, of clear desires, winged,
meant to soar, have liberty for its nest.
It would forget man moves about in chains.
It put valour and oblivion where feathers failed.

Sometimes it rose so high, the sky shone
over the skin, under the skin the bird.
Being which one day you confused with a lark
you fell next day heavy as hailstone.

Ya sabes que las vidas de los demás son losas
con que tapiarte: cárceles con que tragar la tuya.
Pasa, vida, entre cuerpos, entre rejas hermosas.
A través de las rejas, libre la sangre afluya.

Triste instrumento alegre de vestir; apremiante
tubo de apetecer y respirar el fuego.
Espada devorada por el uso constante.
Cuerpo en cuyo horizonte cerrado me despliego.

No volarás. No puedes volar, cuerpo que vagas
por estas galerías donde el aire es mi nudo.
Por más que te debatas en ascender, naufragas.
No clamarás. El campo sigue desierto y mudo.

Los brazos no aletean. Son acaso una cola
que el corazón quisiera lanzar al firmamento.
La sangre se entristece de debatirse sola.
Los ojos vuelven tristes de mal conocimiento.

Cada ciudad, dormida, despierta loca, exhala
un silencio de cárcel, de sueño que arde y llueve
como un élitro ronco de no poder ser ala.
El hombre yace. El cielo se eleva. El aire mueve.

136

SEPULTURA DE LA IMAGINACIÓN

Un albañil quería... No le falta aliento.
Un albañil quería, piedra tras piedra, muro
tras muro, levantar una imagen al viento
desencadenador en el futuro.

Quería un edificio capaz de lo más leve.
No le faltaba aliento. ¡Cuánto aquel ser quería!
Piedras de plumas, muros de pájaros los mueve
una imaginación al mediodía.

You know the lives of others to be slabs
to wall you up; gaols that will swallow your life.
Life, move on among bodies, among pretty bars.
Through the bars may the blood flow free.

Sad tool, glad to be clothed; pipe
with the urge to savour, breathe fire.
Sword eaten away by constant use.
Body in whose closed horizon I unfold.

You will not fly. You cannot fly, body that wander
about these corridors whose air knot me down.
May you so struggle to rise, you crash.
You must not cry out. The field stays clear and silent.

Your arms don't flutter. They might be a tail,
which your heart should wish could curl up the sky.
Your blood is saddened to struggle all alone.
Your eyes come back desolate for poor knowledge.

Every city that slept wakes up in madness, it exhales
a prison's hush, a sleep on fire which drums
raucously like the sheath of the wing it itself could not become.
The man lies prone. The sky rises. The air moves.

136

BURIAL OF THE IMAGINATION

A mason wanted ... He did not lack the grit.
A mason wanted ... Stone after stone, one well
after another, to raise a likeness to the wind,
unleashing agency to come.

He meant an edifice to hold what is lightest.
He did not lack the grit. He wanted that so much!
A noonday fancy moves feathery stones
and walls that birds make up.

Reía. Trabajaba. Cantaba. De sus brazos,
con un poder más alto que el ala de los truenos,
iban brotando muros lo mismo que aletazos.
Pero los aletazos duran menos.

Al fin, era la piedra su agente. Y la montaña
tiene valor de vuelo si es totalmente activa.
Piedra por piedra es peso y hunde cuanto acompaña
aunque esto sea un mundo de ansia viva.

Un albañil quería… Pero la piedra cobra
su torva densidad brutal en un momento.
Aquel hombre labraba su cárcel. Y en su obra
fueron precipitados él y el viento.

137

ETERNA SOMBRA

Yo que creí que la luz era mía
precipitado en la sombra me veo.
Ascua solar, sideral alegría
ígnea de espuma, de luz, de deseo.

Sangre ligera, redonda, granada:
raudo anhelar sin perfil ni penumbra.
Fuera, la luz en la luz sepultada.
Siento que sólo la sombra me alumbra.

Sólo la sombra. Sin rastro. Sin cielo.
Seres. Volúmenes. Cuerpos tangibles
dentro del aire que no tiene vuelo,
dentro del árbol de los imposibles.

Cárdenos ceños, pasiones de luto.
Dientes sedientos de ser colorados.
Oscuridad del rencor absoluto.
Cuerpos lo mismo que pozos cegados.

He laughed. He worked. He sang. Out of his arms,
with a might loftier than thunder's wing,
walls were springing as would wingbeats.
Only wingbeats last shorter.

After all, the stone was his means. And the mountain
is as good as the flight, if all of it is active.
Stone by stone it is weighed and it sinks what it serves,
although this be a world of living strife.

A mason wanted ... But stone instantly
retrieves its brutal, scowling thickness.
That man was fashioning his jail. And both
he and the wind were thrown into his work.

137

EVERLASTING DARK

I, who believed light to be mine,
see myself flung into the dark.
Solar ember, sidereal joy,
foam of fire, of flash, of desire.

Weightless, round, ripe blood:
swift yearning without profile or penumbra.
Outside light buried in light.
I feel the dark alone illuminating me.

The dark alone. Traceless. Skyless.
Beings. Shapes. Tangible bodies,
within the flightless air,
within the tree of what cannot be.

Purple brows, mourning passions.
Teeth that thirst to redden.
Darkness of absolute rancour.
Bodies as choked as wells.

Falta el espacio. Se ha hundido la risa.
Ya no es posible lanzarse a la altura.
El corazón quiere ser más de prisa
fuerza que ensancha la estrecha negrura.

Carne sin norte que va en oleada
hacia la noche siniestra, baldía.
¿Quién es el rayo de sol que la invada?
Busco. No encuentro ni rastro del día.

Sólo el fulgor de los puños cerrados,
el resplandor de los dientes que acechan.
Dientes y puños de todos los lados.
Más que las manos, los montes se estrechan.

Turbia es la lucha sin sed de mañana.
¡Qué lejanía de opacos latidos!
Soy una cárcel con una ventana
ante una gran soledad de rugidos.

Soy una abierta ventana que escucha,
por donde ver tenebrosa la vida.
Pero hay un rayo de sol en la lucha
que siempre deja la sombra vencida.

Space fails. Laughter has sunk.
One can no longer soar in the high.
The heart will be more quickly
a force to widen the narrow black.

Northless surge of flesh dashing
towards sinister, barren night.
Who will, sunbeam-like, enter it?
I search. I find no trace of day.

Only the glare of tight fists,
the glint of stalking teeth.
Teeth and fists on all sides.
It is not hands but mountains are squeezed.

Turbid is the thirstless struggle for a tomorrow
Such a remoteness of opaque heartbeats!
I am a jail with a single window
that opens on a great howling solitude.

I am an open, listening window
through which to watch tenebrous life.
But there is in the combat a sun ray
that always moves on over a defeated dark.

E

POEMAS TACHADOS EN EL CANCIONERO DE AUSENCIAS
1

Duérmete, pena.
Déjame dormir.
Pena de marzo.
Dolor de abril.
Ansia de mayo,
de no tenerte aquí.

2

CASA CERRADA

El hijo muerto no cierra las puertas.
El marido ausente, sí.
Ausentes del corazón,
ausentes de mí.

3

Yo solo.
Entre estas cuatro paredes
yo solo y un volcán.
Nadie nos apagará.
Yo solo.
Yo solo sobre este lecho
de escarcha, y mi volcán.
Nadie nos apagará.

E

POEMS REJECTED FROM THE
SONGBOOK OF ABSENCES

1

Go to sleep, sorrow.
Let me sleep.
Sorrow of March.
Pain of April.
Desire of May,
not to have you here.

2

CLOSED HOUSE

The dead son doesn't close doors.
The absent husband does.
Both absent from the heart.
Both absent from me.

3

I alone.
Within these four walls
I alone and a volcano.
No one will quench us.
I alone.
I alone upon this bed
all frost, and my volcano.
No one will quench us.

4

Ausente, ausente,
ausente lejano.
Dame desde lejos
carta de tu mano,
sangre de tu puño y letra,
calor de tu cuerpo humano.

5

MI CUERPO

Mi cuerpo sin tu cuerpo,
canal que un palo seco,
tendido en una sábana
de mármoles y desiertos.

¡Qué triste un cuerpo solo!

Mi cuerpo sin el tuyo,
como un ojo sin otro,
brumoso de rocío,
temblando siempre otoño.

¡Qué triste un cuerpo solo!

6

Encadena mis ojos,
clávame las manos
que detrás de tu sombra
se van clamando.

Átame con tu pelo,
clávame con los clavos
suaves de tus pestañas,
distantes que no alcanzo.

4

Absent, absent,
absent faraway.
From far away give me
a letter from your own hand,
the blood of your own handwriting,
the warmth of your human body.

5

MY BODY

Without your body, my body,
a channel, a dead log
stretched on a marble
and wasteland sheet.

How sad a lone body!

My body without yours,
like one eye without its twin,
mist-bedewed,
ever quivering in the autumn.

How sad a lone body!

6

Chain my eyes,
nail my hands
and crying out they'll go
in your shadow's pursuit.

Tie me with your hair,
nail me with the nails
of those soft, distant eyelashes
of yours beyond my reach.

7

¿Cuándo vas a volver?
¡Cuando sean gusanos
las manzanas de ayer!

8

El hijo primero,
primera alegría.
Primer desengaño.
Primer ataúd
que estrecho en mis brazos,
que deja mi casa
sangrando.

9

Se puso el sol.
Pero tu temprano vientre
de nuevo se levantó
por el Oriente.

10

Te escribo y el sol
palpita en la tinta.

¡Ausencia viva!

Te espero… La lluvia
se ciñe a mi espera.

¡Ausencia muerta!

7

When will you come back?
when yesterday's apples
will be all worms!

8

The first son,
a first joy.
First heartbreak.
First casket
that I press between my arms,
that leaves my house
bleeding.

9

The sun set.
But your early womb
rose again
on the Orient.

10

I write to you, and the sun
throbs in the ink.

Living absence!

I await you ... The rain
binds my waiting.

Dead absence!

11

Nadie se da cuenta
de estos zapatos,
junto a los que corro
y caigo.

Nadie se da cuenta
de estas ropas
junto a las que vela
y llora.

12

¿Qué aguardas, mesa?
¿Qué esperas, silla?
¿Para quién seguís en pie?
Para aquella lejanía.

13

El sol y la luna quieren
que nunca nos separemos.
Nunca. Pero el tiempo.

¿Y de qué está el tiempo hecho
si no de soles y lunas?

Pero el tiempo… Nunca.

14

Este molino donde
el árabe molía
parece un recuerdo
de la sangre mía,
dorado en la noche,
dorado en el día.

11

No one notices
these shoes
near which I run
and fall.

No one notices
these clothes
near which she watches
and cries.

12

What is it you are waiting for, table?
What is it you are waiting for, chair?
Who keeps you on your feet?
That distant thing.

13

It's the will of sun and moon
that we never separate.
Never. But time ...

And what's time made of
if not of suns and moons?

But time .... Never.

14

This mill in which
the Arab milled
resembles a memory
of my own blood
golden by night,
golden by day.

15

Sobre el cuerpo de la luna
nadie pone su calor.
Frente a frente sol y luna
entre la luna y el sol
que se buscan y no se hallan
    tú y yo.
Pero por fin se hallarán
nos hallaremos, amor,
y el mundo será redondo
hacia nuestro corazón.

16

Me tendí en la arena
para que el mar me enterrara,
me dejara, me cogiera,
¡ay de la ausencia!

15

Upon the moon's body
no one lays any warmth.
Face to face sun and moon:
between the moon and the sun,
that search and can't find each other,
    you and I.
They'll find each other at last.
Love, we shall find each other,
and the world will be round
as it points to our heart.

16

I stretched out on the sand
for the sea to bury me,
to leave me, to pick me up,
ah, absence.

About the Translator

A member of Aosdána, the Irish National Academy of Artists, Michael Smith was the first Writer-in-Residence to be appointed by University College, Dublin. He is a poet who has given a lifetime of service to the art of poetry both in English and Spanish. He has been described as a classical modernist, a poet of modern life. Born in Dublin in 1942, Smith was the founder of New Writers' Press in 1967 and has been responsible for the publication of over seventy books and magazines. He was founder and editor of the influential literary magazine *The Lace Curtain*. From 1984 to 1989 he was a member of the Arts Council. He has translated into English and published some of the most difficult and exhilarating poets in Spanish, including Federico García Lorca, Pablo Neruda, Miguel Hernández (*Unceasing Lightning*) and the two great Spanish masters of the baroque, Francisco de Quevedo and Luis de Góngora. He has also translated Gerardo Diego's *Manual de espumas*, a *Selected Poems* of José Hierro and selections of the poems of Jiménez and Luis Cernuda, among others. In 2001 he received the prestigious translating award, the European Academy Medal, for his translation of great Spanish poets. His own poetry has appeared in numerous anthologies of Irish poetry, including *The Penguin Book of Contemporary Irish Poetry*. Among his two most recent books are *The Purpose of the Gift: Selected Poems* and *Maldon and Other Translations* (NWP/Shearsman). His poetry has been translated into Spanish, Polish, French and German.

Lightning Source UK Ltd.
Milton Keynes UK
23 April 2010

153242UK00002B/72/P